Mike & Shareen,

Thanks again for your generosity &
time in taking the students sailing. They had a
great time! This experience the last 2 years
has been such an effective way to welcome the
freshmen into our high school ministry.

Thanks for your servants spirit and
willingness to serve in so many ways in the
Kingdom!

Pastor Jeff

The American
SAILBOAT

GREGORY O. JONES

MBI Publishing Company

First published in 2002 by MBI Publishing Company, Galtier Plaza, Suite 200, 380 Jackson Street, St. Paul, MN 55101-3885 USA

MBI Publishing Company books are also available at discounts in bulk quantity for industrial or sales-promotional use. For details write to Special Sales Manager at Motorbooks International Wholesalers & Distributors, Galtier Plaza, Suite 200, 380 Jackson Street, St. Paul, MN 55101-3885 USA.

Library of Congress Cataloging-in-Publication Data Available

ISBN 0-7603-1002-5

Edited by Paul Johnson
Designed by Stephanie Michaud

Printed in China

On the front cover: The Herreshoff Yawl Cat *Aida* is part of the yawl cat tradition that started in during the depression years. *Benjamin Mendlowitz*

On the frontispiece: New York YC members Philip H. and George A. Adee originally owned the New York Thirty *Amorita*, the former *Adelaide II*. Like all its 17 sister ships, the *Amorita* was built between the autumn of 1904 and spring of 1905 at the Herreshoff yard. *Paul Darling*

On the title page: The Shields class, designed by Olin Stephens, is notable, among other things, for its extremely high ballast ratio of over 60 percent and a class rule that allows only one set of sails per season. *Rosenfeld collection, Mystic, Connecticut*

On the back cover: Friendship sloops, blessed with a name that reveals both their place of origin and what any owner will tell you is the nature of the vessel, are a near-perfect example of the transformation of work boat to pleasure boat. *Alison Langley*

Clark Mills' Optimist dinghy, literally a worldwide favorite, was designed in 1947 at the request of the Clearwater, Florida, Optimist Club. The 1950s would not be complete without mentioning this little boat, which became popular internationally almost overnight. Just 7 feet, 6 inches long, Mills designed it so a boatbuilder of average skill could build it from a single sheet of plywood, for less than $50. He was inspired by the sharpie, scaling it down to a kid-size boat. He then donated the design to the Optimist Club, in the interests of fostering sailing. *Peter McGowan*

TABLE OF
Contents

Acknowledgements

This book resulted from a chance conversation with my editor at MBI, Paul Johnson. Had I realized how complex a task it would be to attempt to write the history of American sailboats, even with the limitation of keeping it to a 76-year period, I would have gone sailing instead.

Paul's boundless enthusiasm, patience, and encouragement helped produce this book, almost as much as all the designers, builders and sailors whose work is documented.

The history of the American Sailboat is fragmented and in many cases contradictory. Primary sources disagree as often they agree, and much of the historical record simply doesn't exist any more. Fires, carelessness, and a simple lack of appreciation of something's value to posterity are all to blame for the paucity of material. Sailing still isn't taken seriously except by sailors, but there is much to be learned by reviewing and analyzing the material that still exists. The sport reflects us. It's what we do with our leisure time, and at the risk of over-simplification it is one of the few remaining places where we can confront nature on its own terms.

To all those people I talked with, whose books provided information, to the many photographers, from professionals to the amateurs who had just one photograph but it was the absolutely right one, I offer my thanks. They number literally in the hundreds, from one-design fleet commodores to yacht club members to authors to owners of used book stores to ordinary sailors to curators of maritime museums. The success this book enjoys is entirely theirs. I merely offered them a chance to display their knowledge and skill. Any mistakes, omissions, or errors are entirely mine.

—Gregory O. Jones
Port Washington, Wisconsin, 2001

Introduction

Spend a day on the water anywhere in the United States, from Long Island Sound to the Keys, from the Great Lakes to Puget Sound, and you are part of the American sailing tradition. While the roots of that tradition originated in England, it didn't take long for us to put our unique stamp on sailing.

Sailing for pleasure began with European royalty. But in the United States, sailing was more often connected with work; even though fishing boats often raced each other, it was to get back to port first and command the best prices.

What the nation needed for sailing to become a popular recreation, rather than a means of earning a living, was an economy that allowed leisure time, and a work force with money to spend. In 1900 the frontier was all but gone, and fortunes made building railroads were consolidated. Prices for basic living needs were stable, and the American economy was growing. As a nation we were confident, even brash. Hadn't we invented the telegraph? Spanned the continent with a railroad? Our technology was everywhere, and there seemed to be nothing we couldn't do.

The genius of this country's designers has produced boats that have been preserved almost as works of art, but as functional art, used and loved, like Nora, a 41-foot S&S yawl built in 1962. *Alison Langley*

On the East Coast, sailing for pleasure had existed for decades. Places such as Chesapeake Bay, Long Island Sound, Buzzards Bay, Nantucket Sound, and Cape Cod Bay all had boats crewed by sailors who were there for their own enjoyment. Boats such as the America's Cup J-series kept interest high in big-boat racing, and small one-designs were built, loved, and raced by their owners in great numbers.

Although there were contracts for working boats, Nathanael Herreshoff's yard is best remembered for building boats whose only purpose in life was to provide enjoyment for their owners. The S-class, first built in 1919, was a well-proportioned little sloop of such svelte lines there is no way the boat could have been used for utilitarian purposes. Herreshoff's clients were not the sort of people who modified a working boat by adding berths or a cuddy where once rested a catch box or a net windlass. Over about 10 years of production the Herreshoff yard built upward of 150 boats, the first costing less than $2,000 apiece.

One-designs were often commissioned by yacht clubs interested in a class that would be theirs alone. The boat was usually designed for the conditions of the area, and while classes have come and gone over the years, some are still actively built and raced.

Prior to the fiberglass boat, which appeared shortly after World War II and greatly simplified mass production, wooden boats could still be produced in series. One person would spend the day sawing the planks for a particular part of the boat, say the doghouse, and spend the next day fitting that component to a series of boats.

Production in such places as the Cape Cod Shipbuilding Company's yard involved making batches of ribs or deck planking, thus providing a modicum of production-line–style time savings, but the final work— offering up planks, fitting and nailing or screwing together— still required considerable man-hours. Even though the pieces were cut to the same dimensions, there were slight variations arising from hand construction. Thus, no two boats of this period were identical in the way that modern craft are, where the precise location of screws and other fasteners is as consistent as every other dimension and component.

Wooden boats lent themselves well to home construction and many sailors simply constructed the craft they wanted, rather than shopping for it. In the years prior to fiberglass, boat plans were a hot item among sailors.

Modifying a work boat into a pleasure boat—that etymological shift from "sailboat" to "yacht"—was often a

The Catalina 30 represented a major change in sailboat design and marketing. It wasn't designed as a racer, and didn't promise to take you to the South Seas. Rather, it was a family cruiser-racer, wildly popular and bought by literally thousands. (See chapter 10 for details on the Catalina.)

Tod Balfour

backyard undertaking. The evolution of this process can be seen in boats whose lines mirrored working boats, but were built with the pleasure sailor in mind. From the Barnegat Bay sneakbox to the Chesapeake Bay bugeyes to the various pilot boats and coastal fishing vessels whose lines influenced yacht designers, watercraft for pleasure descended from boats built for work.

Our nation's population in its early years was very coastal, with water transport being easier and faster than the primitive road system. The schooner, that most American of designs, carried cargo and passengers, and in times of war the Navy commissioned private vessels, known as privateers, whose activities were sometimes difficult to distinguish from those more often attributed to pirates. American whalers circled the globe, and the clippers, designed by men such as Donald McKay, set speed records that have only very recently been beaten.

Joshua Slocum, a retired American sea captain, pioneered the idea of circumnavigating for pleasure in the final years of the nineteenth century, and published his seminal book, *Sailing Alone Around the World*, in 1900. It would be another 20 years before an Iowa farm boy, Harry Pidgeon, would duplicate his feat. While Slocum's 36-foot sloop *Spray* was not, strictly speaking, built by him—*Spray* was an upside-down hulk, rotting in a field—Slocum decided the boat fit his finances and went to work on it. Anyone who has taken on a similar task will sympathize with Slocum, and it is safe to say that the boat, for all practical purposes, was home-built.

Pidgeon's 34-foot yawl *Islander* was home-built to a design by Charles D. Mower published in *The Rudder*. He started work in 1917, left in 1921, and returned nearly four years later. When he circumnavigated the globe again in his late 60s, also aboard *Islander*, he was the first person to "tie the global knot" twice.

It is significant that Pidgeon's boat was from a design published in a magazine. *The Rudder* offered a forum for designers that was unique, being open to all, and was both a clearinghouse and an arbiter of nautical design.

American designers, although influenced by foreign, mostly English, designers, were very much their own men (and they were almost entirely men). The conditions along the American coastline were much more varied than those of England, and the designers took this into account when penning their boats.

The reason yachting grew in popularity was the unprecedented growth of a working class with money and leisure time. Nowhere else in the world was this happening quite like it did in the United States, and the absence of a rigid class structure made yachting an imaginable dream for would-be sailors. In England, even the bottoms of the estuaries were owned by the aptly named "landed gentry," and mooring space had to be rented from the local lord. In the United States, land title stopped at the high-water mark, making mooring space available to anyone with the desire to use one.

It helped, of course, that wood was inexpensive. The great forests of Minnesota, Wisconsin, and Michigan were being cut down as fast as the immigrant armies could wield an ax, and in the early parts of the twentieth century there was still a lot of forest available on the eastern seaboard.

Boats were everywhere, despite the vast expanses of prairie and desert. The rivers provided transport, and the Great Lakes were the highway of the Midwest. Along the shores, boats carried cargo, caught fish, dragged for oysters, and carried passengers. Even after the arrival of the transcontinental railroad, far more cargo was carried by sea than by rail.

As yachting grew in popularity, the demand for boats, and the search for new water sports, increased. The large boats raced by the wealthy could attract only a limited number of participants. In order for people of more ordinary means to sail, boats had to be smaller. To provide satisfying sport and make it affordable, boat makers refined techniques for mass production. The need for greater manufacturing output was a major factor behind the introduction and popularity of the one-design.

Francis Sweisguth was the designer responsible for the Star class. He also designed the 18-foot Interlake dinghy, discussed in chapter 4. These Interlake sailors, from the state of Ohio, are part of a sailing scene that is coast to coast and everything in between. *Jeff Thompson*

One-design boats also lent consistency to boat racing, emphasizing sailing skill over design advantage. Yet to many sailors in the early twentieth century, small boats were for boys, whereas men raced big boats—men with big bank accounts, that is. The clubs all had their one-design fleets, but these were raced only within the club. It was very rare, if not unheard of, for a non–club member to own and sail a yacht club's one-design boat.

What was needed was a one-design that transcended the boundaries of yacht club membership. That boat was the Star. Evolved from a 1907 William Gardner design called the Bug, the Star was available to be raced and enjoyed by anyone, club member or not.

On the cruising front, similar things were happening. Yards such as the Cape Cod Shipbuilding Co. began to mass-produce small cruising boats. Magazines, including *The Rudder* and *Forest & Stream,* popularized designs for boats that did not require a hired crew, and the idea of "family cruising," in which the only people on board were the ones who owned the boat, became possible.

The boats that people were sailing then were nearly all made of wood, assembled from various–sized pieces and fastened together with bolts, screws, treenails, and, on boats with metal frames, called "composite" boats, rivets. There were a few boats built of plywood, and a few experiments with canvas covers treated with various chemicals resembling shellacs, but wood was king until after World War II.

There was a brief period when molded plywood appeared to be the next good thing. Hot-molded plywood had been used during the 1940s to build lifeboats and dinghies, but the drawback of that system was the impressive equipment required. Molded plywood did not lend itself to home construction, or even construction by a small yard.

The whole game changed after World War II. Fiberglass resins, developed by the various militaries involved in the war, were well suited to boatbuilding, and as soon as the smoke cleared, wartime energies turned to peaceful pursuits. The introduction in 1947 of two fiberglass boats—the Rebel, a 16-foot daysailer, and the Swan, a 12-1/2-foot catboat—set a benchmark for the future of boat construction. Although it wasn't fully appreciated at the time, these boats, or more precisely, what they were made of, were the future.

At the 1950 New York Boat Show, 22 boats were fiberglass—15 more than at the previous major boat show. Just 11 years later, at the 1961 show, more than half of all boats on exhibit were made of fiberglass, a material that didn't rot, leak, rust, or corrode.

The final obstacle to widespread boat ownership had been removed. The high-maintenance factor of wooden boats, which required the owner to have either time or money to devote to the simple task of keeping a wooden hull watertight, had been eliminated by technology. Boat construction had always required a fair bit of skill on the part of the builders, even under production-line conditions, but fiberglass construction skills were easily learned. Design was still important, even more so, perhaps, as now the design had to incorporate the building methods of fiberglass.

Boats became less expensive, small boats in particular, because they cost less to build. Fiberglass was made in large part from petroleum, which was plentiful and cheap in the United States.

In 1950, the median annual income in the United States was $12,074. In 1952, a brand-new daysailer Rebel cost less than $1,000. For comparison, in 1997, the median income was $18,736, and the 15-foot West Wight Potter daysailer cost $4,000. Many middle-class people took advantage of the low price of boats, taking up sailing in large numbers in the years following World War II.

The first eight decades of the twentieth century will probably be seen as the most vibrant and evolutionary in the history of American yachting. Vastly more people were sailing for pleasure at the end of this period than at the beginning, and while the sport continues to grow, we will never again see the huge increases of those 80 years. It was a wonderful time to be on the water, and those early sailors can be seen now as genuine pioneers, changing the entire social structure of sailing. There will always be the blue-blazer crowd in sailing, but now they are not the only crowd.

The time span of this book, 1900–1976, covers those exciting years when the social and economic changes in this country changed for all time the demography of sailors. In 1976, we were 200 years old, and, just in time for our bicentennial birthday, petroleum prices began climbing, sometimes with dizzying speed. Crude oil, which had been so cheap as to barely be worth considering in the manufacturing processes that used it, suddenly became a serious matter. The raw material of much of the fiberglass boat industry came from wells in countries that suddenly became aware that they controlled the taps, and, therefore, the price of this vital raw material.

The first shocks were felt in 1973, as a result of the Yom Kippur War in the Middle East, when Syria and Egypt attacked Israel. Within six months the price of a barrel of crude oil jumped 400 percent. By 1976, the full effect of this price increase, with more to follow, was felt throughout the industry, and the price of fiberglass boats rose rapidly. It was the end of inexpensive boats; a thousand dollars a foot had been the benchmark price for a fully equipped yacht for some time, and those days were over.

While this book does not cover the America's Cup, although certainly its history involves American sailboats, it spotlights instead the boats sailed by "everyone else." It is to those people that I dedicate this book—the many, the nameless, the enthusiastic; those sailors who made sailing in America what it is today. ✳

From Work to Play

The Birth of Recreational Sailing

*T*he idea of going to sea on a sailboat for pleasure is old enough to have been ridiculed by the English writer Samuel Johnson, who in 1759 compared sailing to being in jail—with the chance of being drowned. Succeeding generations would take a far more favorable view, but to act upon it would require a change in the availability and price of boats: the first had to go up and the second down in large measure. The answer, at first, was to take what was already available—working boats—and turn them to recreational purposes. Boats designed and built for pleasure sailing were a very small part of shipbuilding in general until comparatively recently.

From those work-boat roots grew the sport of recreational sailing, at first by working sailors, or people attracted to boats and with the means to pursue it. Cruising, when done, was an activity for large boats and wealthy people with free time. Working people worked long hours and had virtually no paid holidays.

It took changes in all those areas for sailing to become a sport in which people of ordinary means could participate. While racing on a sailboat, one against another, has been a part of sailing since the second sailboat was launched, structured racing was almost always a sport of the

Fleets of Stars, an Olympic class and the boat that virtually defined the essence of the one-design, are found worldwide. Nearly every sailor competing at the upper levels of the sport has raced a Star at one time in their career, and vast numbers of club-level sailors race them regularly on their home waters.

Reliance, designed by Nat Herreshoff to defend the America's Cup in 1903, beat Shamrock III handily. At 144 feet on deck, its sheer size required a small army to crew the boat. James Burton/ Rosenfeld collection, Mystic, Connecticut

In this famous photograph taken during Cowes Week, 1934, five J-class boats, left to right, Velsheda, Candida, Shamrock V, Astra, and Britannia, head off at the start. There were only 10 J-class boats built, and another six rebuilt to fit the J-class rule. Truly sailing vessels, none of them had engines. Beken of Cowes

moneyed classes—the profoundly moneyed classes. The crews for these boats, whose names ring in the history of yacht racing—*Weetamoe, Astra, Shamrock, Candida, Velsheda,* and others—were hired, and came from the ranks of professional seamen.

These hired crew were usually fishermen, sometimes able-bodied seamen from the world of commercial shipping, and while it is quite likely they enjoyed their days on the water, it was, in the final summation, a job for them. The idea of going to sea for pleasure had to await a time when ordinary working people had the time, money, and above all, the inclination to sail for the pure pleasure of the sensation.

Aspiring sailors without the finances to have a boat built for the express purpose of recreation typically purchased a fishing boat or a similar small working boat, perhaps one used to deliver the pilot to offshore vessels or to deliver supplies.

The field of amateur yacht design was also increasingly active, and several magazines in the era before

World War I had sections devoted to the subject. The now defunct magazine, *Forest & Stream* had a full-time yachting editor, and *The Rudder*, in existence from 1891 to 1950, published designs regularly. The amateur designers most often drew boats suited for cruising; racing boats, especially of the larger sort, were designed by well-funded naval architects, although the amateur still produced successful designs.

THE STAR CLASS BOATS

The first widely accepted racing design that was made for the public, rather than for members of a sponsoring yacht club, was the Star. The Star had its origins in the Bug, designed in 1907 by William Gardner and assisted by a member of Gardner and Company, known only as Mr. Maybrey, in 1907.

The Bug had a fin keel and hard chines, and was actively raced by junior sailors on Manhasset Bay, off Long Island. At that time it was the smallest sloop-rigged sailboat on the water, but at 18 feet overall it was too small for adults to sail. George Corry, properly known as the "Father of the Star," went to Gardner and talked him into adding 5 feet to the design. It was Corry's desire to have a boat suitable for sailors of average means, at a time when small boats were used only as yacht tenders or playthings for boys. Gardner assigned the task to an architect in his office, Francis Sweisguth, and the Star was born.

It was Corry who first put life into the idea that yachting, especially racing, should be available to everyone, regardless of personal finances. Corry's vision was an affordable, one-design boat.

Isaac Smith, of Port Washington, New York, built 22 Stars and the fleet first took to the waters of Long Island Sound in 1911. This fleet cost $260 per boat, which works out to $4,700 in year 2000 dollars.

Later that year, the Green Brothers' yard in Chelsea, Massachusetts, built another 11, and this was the beginning, perhaps, of the eternal argument as to what is a

"true" boat of the class in question. These boats, although built to Gardner's plans, did not become recognized as "real" Stars until 10 years later, after the formation of the International Star Association.

There were other, larger versions built, most notable being the Fish class in 1913, but the larger version did not meet with the success of the "just right" Star. The design became official in 1916, through the efforts of George W. Elder, who bought his first Star in 1914. The Star Class Association of America, almost too grandiose a title for what was at the time a very loosely knit group of enthusiasts, became a reality in 1915.

RACING SPURS GROWTH

The step from local, even national-level racing to international racing was a large one. The Star class organized races locally, between fleets on Long Island Sound and Lake Erie. The presence of the Canadian boats in the Great Lakes was the impetus for the formation of the International Star Class Yacht Racing Association on January 22, 1922, at the Hotel Astor in New York

The Bug class, designed in 1907 by William Gardner, was the forerunner of the Star class and clearly shows the lines that are still used in the Star. On board are George Corry at the helm with Mrs. Corry as crew. *Rosenfeld collection, Mystic, Connecticut*

City. George Corry was named the first president. Elder succeeded him in 1924; Elder proved to be the driving force behind the class' growth.

Part of the reason for the class' success is that it has always been a semidevelopment class, open to evolutionary changes. Because of this, the Star has been a leader in racing design. Initially rigged with a gaff sail, the first bermudan rig was put on a Star belonging to a sailor known as D. H. Cowl in 1918, at a time when the

These early Star boats, still with the gaff rigs, have a significant history. George Corry owned number 17, his *Little Dipper*. *Rosenfeld collection, Mystic, Connecticut*

Today's Stars, more popular than ever, are an Olympic class, and seem destined to remain one. They require a heavy crew, and most of the world's top sailors have been Star sailors. *Peter McGowan*

three-cornered bermudan sail was rarely seen. This first bermudan rig, following the suggestion of Gardner, carried a hollow, curved mast with huge spreaders, and was notably unsuccessful, possibly due to its being sailed by a variety of different skippers unaccustomed to the new rig.

In 1921, however, three sailors rigged their bermudan Stars with thin, straight masts, with a pronounced aft rake, and began winning races. By the end of the

next sailing season, the four-cornered gaff sail was an endangered species, due in part to the fact that the original high-peaked gaff sail was easily modified into the bermudan shape.

It was truly the Star that changed the face of sailboat racing, with the introduction of a class transcending the boundaries of club membership or even national background. The Star wasn't a work boat that had been taken out of service for use as a pleasure yacht; it was designed as a pleasure boat, and in the early twentieth century, that was almost a revolutionary step.

THE BIRTH OF CRUISING

With small-boat racing now within the grasp of ordinary citizens, cruising had to follow. At the turn of the century, boat yards for the most part still relied on

Hanging out on the boards, *Flying Cloud*'s crew strikes a delicate balance. Note the sheets, attached to the club, and the wishbones.

Marc Castelli

Today's Star boats carry sail controls and adjustments, which were unheard of when the class began, but the boat itself would be recognized as a Star by George Corry himself. *Peter McGowan*

the large commissions of wealthy sailors desiring a larger or faster boat. Yards did build small boats, of course, but a sailor who could afford only a small boat often couldn't afford to have it made. If a sailor wanted a small boat, an affordable boat, home building was usually the answer. In this pursuit, the working-class sailor had a champion in the form of Thomas Fleming Day, the editor of *The Rudder* and so outspoken in his views that he attracted the attention of L. Francis Herreshoff, who, in speaking of the egalitarian notions that

Day held in yachting, said that Day "was a boatman at heart, not a yachtsman or a racer."

Day was all three, of course; he merely didn't fit the pattern of yachtsmen of the time, most particularly the wealthy ones whose large, expensive boats were the mainstay of yacht clubs and the social circles of the moneyed classes. Day organized the first ocean race for small boats, with none of the six entered vessels longer than 30 feet. His gaff yawl *Sea Bird*, which he designed to be built by the owner, was only 19 feet on the waterline.

With its hard chines and comparatively simple lines, it was a good choice for the amateur builder.

Another magazine writer of the time, Alfred F. Loomis, popularized the idea of going to sea in small boats, although many of his early adventures were in powerboats—a decision driven as much by advertiser influence on *Motorboat*, his magazine, as any innate desire to forsake sailing.

Also on the staff of *Motorboat* at that time was William W. Nutting, who made several well-documented ocean cruises aboard his 28-foot cutter, including a single-handed cruise to Newfoundland.

Loomis sailed a small yawl to Panama, the voyage on which he learned the art of sailing. He wrote a book about it—*The Cruise of the Hippocampus*—which was rewarded with instant success and gave credence to the concept of sailing small boats on the open sea.

The role of magazines in publicizing this idea cannot be overestimated. When, in 1920, Nutting commissioned a young William Atkin to design a 45-foot ketch named *Typhoon* and proceeded to sail it across the Atlantic, in his words, "for the fun of it," there was a palpable sea change in other sailors' perceptions of this sort of activity.

—THE CRUISING CLUB OF AMERICA—

The number of sailors lacking silver spoons at birth was growing, but there was no organization reflecting this fact. Sailing clubs had been nearly the exclusive domain of the wealthy class, whose members owned yachts that matched their finances. A club for "real sailors" didn't exist—not, at least, in Nutting's mind. He organized the Cruising Club of America (CCA) in 1922, with the motto "nowhere is too far." The idea had come to him after his arrival in England

aboard *Typhoon*, where he was feted by members of the Royal Cruising Club. Founding members included the designer, John Alden. Among the honorary members was Day, who with Loomis and Nutting had made many voyages of the sort exemplary of the CCA's goals.

Nutting was the first commodore, followed by Herbert Stone, the publisher of *Yachting* magazine. The forming of the CCA marked a turning point as significant as the founding of the Star Class Association, making fact of the demographic shift in boat ownership and use in the United States.

With the formation of a club, and magazines that promoted cruising (and racing) on small boats, where

Rainbow, Cornelius Vanderbilt's New York Seventy, featured the new cross-cut sails developed by Nat Herreshoff. The new sails were made possible with better, long-staple Egyptian cotton sailcloth and improved sailmaking techniques. *Rosenfeld collection, Mystic, Connecticut*

New York YC members Philip H. and George A. Adee originally owned the New York 30 *Amorita*, the former *Adelaide II*. The *Amorita* was built at the Herreshoff yard. *Paul Darling*

did that leave big boats? There were, naturally, fewer of them, but the idea of designing boats to a single design, or class, was taking hold even in the bigger boats. The New York Yacht Club commissioned the design of a sloop with a 70-foot waterline in 1900, but even in those pre–income tax years, only four of them were built, all by the Herreshoff yard. Reducing the waterline length to 50 feet increased the fleet to nine, and there were even more of the 40-foot class built.

A boat called *Minerva* dominated the 40-footers, which were first built in the last years of the nineteenth century. In an effort to beat *Minerva*, bigger boats were built, but again, cost was an issue. The big boats cost their owners an estimated $3,000 (equal to $61,000 in 2000) per crewmember per season, and so the trend was to smaller boats, even for the wealthy. This had the side effect of making boats available to those of lesser means, and so classes with a greater number of boats were possible.

In 1916, the Herreshoff yard launched the first of the 40s, built for both cruising and racing. Critics stated that Herreshoff had taken the design from the Cup boat *Resolute*, and they criticized it for "dumpiness," a result of the headroom and the decidedly un-Herreshoff high free-board. The high rig, coupled with high deadrise that ran for the length of the boat, caused the boat to make what a writer in *Rudder* described as a "slide off to leeward."

The 40s were beamy; they carried the same beam as the 50, although they were 10 feet less on the waterline.

As an indication of the shift from professional crews to owner-sailed boats, the New York YC rules for the 40-foot class limited the number of professional crew to four, allowing two more to be put on temporarily for a race. The owner was required to helm the boat "except on runs and reaches," which left a loophole big enough . . . well, big enough to sail a boat through.

Also forbidden was purchasing more than one set of sails per season, except for replacing sails that "in the opinion of the Committee, may be damaged through accident beyond serviceable repair."

The New York 30, smaller yet, was part of the trend to smaller, owner-driven boats. The ideal of the "Corinthian," the amateur who sailed strictly for the love of the sport, was gaining strength and popularity, given that it made it more difficult for money to beat talent.

The 30s, dating to 1905, were 43 feet overall (the numbers of this series referred to the waterline length), while the later 50s, dating to 1913, were 72 feet overall.

At the beginning of the twentieth century, a 30-foot boat was the smallest boat a member of the New York YC could own and still be eligible to vote on club business. There has been speculation that this was the impetus for Nat Herreshoff's design of the 30, which was criticized, with some accuracy, as being wet and narrow, with a tiller that seemed to always be in the way in the tiny cockpit. It was popular nonetheless, probably to some extent because of the lower costs associated with a smaller boat.

─────── THE SMALL BOAT TREND ───────

The trend—despite the 50s being designed later than the 30—was to smaller, and therefore less expensive, boats. A 50 cost $17,000 in 1913 dollars ($294,000 today), whereas the 30 was "only" $4,000 ($69,000). Nonetheless, the trend was clear. A New York 50 carried a professional crew of only four. Although one of these four was a steward, with, presumably, duties on

(*previous page*) Rugosa II, the last of the New York 40s, was built as a yawl-rigged version of the Herreshoff design in 1926, using the original molds. *Paul Darling*

Nat Herreshoff was justly proud of the New York 50s design, stating they were built of "about the best material and workmanship that ever went into yachts of their size." Despite this, only nine were built, and after World War I many of them were rerigged as yawls or schooners, reducing the size of individual sails and making them easier to handle. This photograph shows two of the fleet, with their gaff topsails set at the start of a prewar race. *Rosenfeld collection, Mystic, Connecticut*

deck as well, such a small professional crew was nearly revolutionary. Even for the wealthy, the wind was blowing in the direction of amateur crews, with the owner taking an increasing role in the boat's sailing.

Instrumental in this switch to the Corinthian ideal was the Seawanhaka Corinthian Yacht Club, whose "rule," discussed in chapter 2, leveled the playing field by providing a set of measurements to which a boat would be built. While far from perfect, the idea was sound.

Along the East Coast, the boats sailed by ordinary people who wished to sail only for pleasure were similar, to the extent that they were evolved from working boats. The New York sloop, as it has been called, was a type of fishing vessel used in the New York–Long Island area, with a centerboard, shallow draft, and an easily handled single-mast gaff rig.

From this boat evolved the sandbagger relatives of this boat could be seen working in areas as disparate as San Francisco Bay, the Gulf of Mexico, and nearly the length of the Atlantic coast. As the sandbagger turned into a pleasure boat, the style spread from coast to coast. The catboat held out in the Cape Cod area, descended as it was from working vessels used in the area of Narragansett Bay.

One of the sandbagger's virtues was its extreme simplicity. In most of its manifestations, the gaff mainsail had a boom that extended beyond the transom, and forward, a boom stuck out practically as far as the boom extended aft. The cockpit had a U-shaped seat around its perimeter, and there was room in it for the large crew. A large crew was paramount. These beamy boats, while possessing a fair bit of initial form stability, were totally reliant upon the crew (or the eponymous sandbags) to remain upright. Sandbags were shifted at the tack, balancing the massive sail area with human ballast.

On Chesapeake Bay, log canoes—working boats descended from the single-log dugouts of the Native Americans—were the working boats used by oystermen,

but enlarged by adding a log to each side, and then, later, more logs, becoming a three- or five-log canoe. They were exceedingly tender, and were balanced by shifting ballast or cargo. Inevitably, the Chesapeake watermen raced them, at first with their catch back to port, but also for the sheer thrill of racing.

As log canoes were replaced by powered craft for the working watermen, log canoes were purchased by sailors who went out on them for pleasure, and, without the ballast of oysters to keep them upright, the use of boards evolved, commensurate with an increase in the sail area.

Log canoes were being built well into the twentieth century, the later ones almost always for pleasure boating; a rich tradition of racing log canoes continues to this day on the Chesapeake.

───────────── CATBOATS ─────────────

Catboats had their adherents, as mentioned, in the Cape Cod area. Boats we would recognize as the forebears of the modern catboat first appeared in the years after the Civil War, and by the 1900s were commonly used in the fishing industry. The rig differed considerably from that of the sandbagger, but was conceptually similar in its stark simplicity. Whereas the sandbagger carried a jib and a main, the catboat had but one sail and a long boom, usually on a short mast mounted well forward in the boat. There was no room for a jib, or even a headstay.

The main was moderate in size, and the mast was nearly always unstayed, that is, no shrouds running from amidships or the stern assisting in holding it upright.

The mast, therefore, was rather thick, and the boom, at least in the earlier boats, rarely went much past the transom. The Cape Cod catboats were beamy, rounded in plan, with a flat bottom and a centerboard. The beam-to-length ratio was even more extreme than that seen on sandbaggers, but with less sail area and a shorter mast, the catboat was much more stable than the sandbagger.

Hull shapes such as those seen in the catboat derive much of their stability from their form, rather than from

Log canoes are still racing today. John Harrison built *Jay Dee* in 1931 and this photograph shows its impossibly tall rig and the trademark opposed wishbones keeping the main and mizzen taut. *Jay Dee* has two crew out on the boards, with the rest of the crew ready to scamper out to keep the boat upright. *Marc Castelli*

the weight of the keel or ballast. As a hull with form stability is heeled, more water is displaced on the leeward side, thus providing resistance to further heeling. As the hull goes farther over, however, there is progressively less additional displacement. Without a weighted keel to stabilize the boat, the limit of stability of a centerboard boat comes rather suddenly, and when a centerboarder reaches that point, a capsize can occur with great rapidity.

The shape of the sandbagger hull provided a fair bit of form stability, but the greater sail area required the use of ballast, in the form of sandbags.

The Cape Cod catboats, despite sharing the stability limitations of the sandbagger, were inherently more stable than the sandbaggers. Their sail areas were less,

but with the steady and often gusty winds of the area, this was more of an advantage than a problem.

Catboats were easy to sail, and could be operated single-handedly, without having to move around bags of sand, or buckets of fish or oysters.

Under the influence of the Seawanhaka Corinthian YC, and particularly its rule, the scow became popularized among the racing class, especially those who sailed in protected waters, fighting for the Seawanhaka Cup. The scow form, resulting in part from a "revolution" against the bigger schooners, produced light, inexpensive, fast boats, using centerboards or sometimes bilge boards (twin boards, offset from the centerline and providing a larger surface area to the water when heeled) that were

Rugosa II, built in 1926, is

the last of the New York

40s, now owned by Halsey

Herreshoff, grandson of

Nathanael Herreshoff.

Paul Darling

also easy to transport. They were commonly carried to races in a horse-drawn wagon, thus becoming what was probably the first trailerable boat.

The full story on the development of the scows is covered in chapter 4. The interaction of the sailors in the inland lakes and those of the Seawanhaka Corinthian YC in the development of this type of boat is unique.

The scows of the Seawanhaka Corinthian YC could be built for as little as $600, a far cry from the thousands that went into larger boats, and with the Seawanhaka Cup being contested internationally in a regular series of matches with Canadian clubs, the thrill of serious international competition was available to a wide range of sailors.

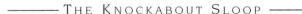

THE KNOCKABOUT SLOOP

As with any rule, eventually the scows developed into rule-beating "freaks," criticized by many for their instability, despite their speed. The boats became usable only on the race course, and this set the scene for the Knockabout sloop, first seen in the area of Marblehead, Massachusetts, in the very last years of the nineteenth century.

The first two Knockabouts were stoutly built, 25 feet, 6 inches overall. The Knockabout could be safely sailed by one person, and there was room for several friends, thus overcoming most of the problems with the scows. They were priced right; early models sold for $300, and they were intended, and designed, for pleasure.

The keel had an iron ballast, an external rudder hung from a sloping transom, and the keel had considerable drag to it, in the style familiar to work boats designed to cope with seas.

A knockabout, strictly speaking, is a small keelboat, with a jib and main, but no bowsprit. Eager sailors built knockabouts by designers from Sam Crocker to Winthrop Warner. The boats were one of the early designs that sprang from the desire for a boat strictly for pleasure, rather than a work boat that had been "decommissioned" and become a yacht.

With these boats, the transition had been fully made: boats were being designed for ordinary people who wished to sail for the sheer pleasure of it.

Another change was that the smaller boats were now being designed for adults. Yes, the Star was an adult boat, but the Snipe, a William Crosby design, at 15 feet, 6 inches, came out in 1931, followed by the C. Lowndes Johnson–designed 16-foot Comet class in 1932. Smaller boats had often been thought of as boats for the "junior" class, (i.e., designed to teach children to sail so they could "graduate" to adult boats).

Two other dinghy classes deserve brief mention here, both by Sparkman & Stephens. The 19-foot Lightning, as good a multipurpose dinghy as has been designed, hit the water in 1938 and is still immensely popular, both for racing and daysailing with family and friends.

Ten years later, the 11-foot Blue Jay, popular with yacht clubs everywhere for the junior class, was designed as a beginner's boat and has a fond spot reserved for it in the hearts of many of today's sailors.

RACING DRIVES DEVELOPMENT

Racing was the crucible for development, in big boats and small. The New York Yacht Club–class boats,

The Comet, mostly an East Coast boat at the time of its introduction, was a strong racing class almost from its introduction. This picture, dated 1927 in the Rosenfeld files, is almost certainly of a later date, as the Comet wasn't designed until 1932. Rosenfeld collection, Mystic, Connecticut

filled with lakes, many of which had their own fleets, usually scows.

The Chicago–Macinac Race, begun in 1898, is 331 miles of freshwater racing that has been immensely popular, attracting ocean racers and freshwater sailors alike. The race has been the occasion for more than one ocean sailor to realize that the Great Lakes are more than a backyard pond, with the same opportunity for mishaps, derring-do, and steep learning curves afforded by the ocean.

With one-designs of all sizes being built for racing and cruising, and designs such as the Knockabout being built for those relaxing afternoons or short cruises, sailing had entered a new age. The new materials—aluminum, plywood, Dacron, and fiberglass—played a significant role in this, but the dominant characteristic of the new sailing age was boats designed and constructed for pleasure, rather than work. It was a new era, but it took decades to dawn. ✳

the 50s, 40s, and 30s, were more in the line of large day-sailers, not intended for the open ocean, although they were used there, sometimes with considerable success. Fast ocean-going vessels became a center of development with the growth of ocean racing. While this book is not a history of that part of sailboating's history, a mention is in order.

The Bermuda Race, first held in 1906, was revived with vigor in 1923, with 22 entries. The winning boat, in 1923 and 1924, interestingly, was a New York YC 40 called *Memory,* rerigged as a jib-headed yawl.

The Transpac, also begun in 1906 and called The Honolulu race at the time, heralded the West Coast's entry into what had been a largely East Coast sport, and the great expanse of land in between the two coasts was

Establishing the Sport of Sailing

Early American Yacht Clubs

*T*he first American yacht club to emphasize small-boat racing was the Seawanhaka Corinthian Yacht Club, located on Center Island in Oyster Bay, New York. The club sponsored the design of a 21-foot boat that was probably the first one-design class. Yacht designer (today he would be called "naval architect") A. Cary Smith drew the design, a club member who was just 21 years old.

The Seawanhaka Cup, awarded beginning in 1895, was the first cup specifically for small boats. These boats were distinct from larger racing vessels in that their owners typically participated in the race. Yacht racing, as done by the "gentleman sailors" of the time, was often a spectator sport for the boat owner. He would watch the race from the luxury of his steam yacht as a hired crew—certainly a hired skipper—and a purchased boat competed against other wealthy men's boats. While yacht owners sometimes sailed, that was a rarity.

The Seawanhaka Corinthian YC changed all that. The club was founded in 1871, and the word "Corinthian" was added to the name in 1881. Then, just as now, the term indicated a sailor who raced a boat as a genuine amateur (i.e., an unpaid participant). The concept was not immediately popular, or even understood. The wealthy sailors of the time wondered aloud "how gentlemen could demean themselves by performing the work which they paid their servants to do." But this was precisely the attraction.

Herreshoff's Bar Harbor 31 was part of a series of racer-cruisers he designed in the years before World War I. This is

Desperate Lark, one of the 13 boats of this class built by the Herreshoff yard in the winter of 1902–1903. *Alison Langley*

The 6-meter *Jill*, by S&S in 1931, was designed to race, and shows the overhangs and hull form typical of the meter classes. *Beken of Cowes*

the world. The cup made its first foreign home in Canada, and was subsequently won by Norway, Scotland, and, at times, by the United States.

From the beginning, until shortly before World War I, races were held using boats called "half-raters," measuring some 15 feet on the waterline.

Enthusiasm for this boat gradually faded, and by 1922 club members observed that there hadn't been a half-rater race since 1910. In an effort to revive the spirit and appeal of small-boat competition, the club designated the 6-meter class as the Seawanhaka Cup boat. The 6-meter boat, a European design, was new to U.S. sailors, but the design was quickly accepted as an affordable racing class. With races held in clubs around the country—indeed, across the globe—this size made transporting the boats to competitions easier. Another advantage of the strict one-design philosophy was that visiting sailors could use local boats, since, theoretically at least, the boats were all the same.

There was, however, a fair bit of leeway in the meter boats, since the number was derived from a calculation involving the sums of the length and the sail area. Longer boats had less sail area, shorter boats more. For example, in the 1927 Seawanhaka Cup series, the sail area of the competing 6-meter boats varied from 450 to 521 square feet, and the length from 31 feet to nearly 37 feet.

In the early years of the Seawanhaka Corinthian YC, New York 30s were fairly popular, with club members actively racing 6 of the 18 boats built. They were raced as a class until the 1920s.

More popular boats were the New York 50s, which were introduced in the summer of 1913. Again, six of these boats were raced, but that constituted two-thirds of the total production of nine boats. Despite the "Corinthian" part of the Seawanhaka Corinthian YC's name, the 50s often had some paid crew, usually consisting of a captain, two crewmembers, and a steward. They were even more expensive to race, a fact some of

William T. Swan, the club's first commodore, put it very well in his farewell speech, charging fellow members to "prosecute vigorously the popularization of Corinthian races with which Seawanhaka is so closely identified." Swan felt that these races were a great source of strength for the club and also "the only true and enjoyable kind of racing."

In 1895, the club sponsored a trophy, to be called the Seawanhaka Corinthian Yacht Club International Challenge Cup. It promptly became known as simply the Seawanhaka Cup. As the name implies, the race was intended as an international challenge, open to boats from around

the wealthy took more notice of after the passage of the Sixteenth Amendment—and resulting income tax—in 1913.

The 50s were large: 50 feet on the waterline with the overhangs stretching the overall length to 72 feet, with a beam of 14 feet, 6 inches and a draft of 9 feet, 8 inches. They were originally rigged as gaff sloops, with club topsails.

E. Townsend, a Seawanhaka Corinthian YC member, owned one of the best of those New York 50s, *Pleione*. The boat at times was rigged as both a sloop and a schooner. It was a particularly successful boat, winning the Astor Cup four times and the King's Cup in its later years, in 1947.

Although the big boats were popular, it was in the smaller classes that the Seawanhaka club really made its mark in history. At the turn of the twentieth century,

club members received a pamphlet outlining the specifications of the Knockabout and the Raceabout classes. It was an attempt at a one-design, but the specifications left much to the designer. For the Knockabouts, the boat was required to have a keel, jib, and mainsail; in accordance with its definition as a Knockabout there was no bowsprit, and the sail area was limited to 500 square feet.

For the Raceabouts, the club was slightly more specific. Centerboards were permitted, and the waterline was limited to 21 feet, with a minimum displacement of 5,900 pounds and a sail area not to exceed 600 square feet. Bowsprits were permitted, a 9-foot oar was required to be carried aboard, and of the three-person crew, the helmsman had to be an amateur.

The club announced a regular series of races for the Raceabout class, to be held every Saturday, and for the first season, 1900, there were seven boats in the fleet.

The New York 50s reveled in a good breeze, and provided plenty of rail-down action for the crews. *Spartan*, like its nine sister ships, was built in 1912 at the Herreshoff yard in Bristol, Rhode Island. *Rosenfeld collection, Mystic, Connecticut*

The Herreshoff Fish class survives to this day. Herreshoff drew the Fish on the lines of his 12-1/2, enlarging them to the Fish's 20-foot, 9-inch length (16 feet on the waterline). *Alison Langley*

With the specifications so open, the two classes attracted the attention of various designers. Clinton Crane, a Seawanhaka Corinthian YC member, turned his hand to designing for the classes. For that first season, he designed one of the Raceabouts, *Raider*, for his brother, H. M. Crane.

There were Raceabout fleets at other clubs as well. The Beverly Yacht Club of Buzzards Bay raced them, calling them "21-footers." Races were organized against the Seawanhaka Corinthian YC—in 1902, for example, a three-race series in August was held at Newport, Rhode Island, that being a halfway point where the fleets could meet. The Seawanhaka Corinthian YC towed its fleet there with larger boats, notably Commodore James' brigantine, *Aloha,* and Vice-Commodore Sloane's auxiliary schooner, *Idler.* The crews of the Raceabouts lived aboard the palatial "towboats" for the duration of the regatta. In this contest H. M. Crane skippered another of his brother's boats, *Whistlewing.*

The results of that first regatta are interesting. Although the Seawanhaka Corinthian YC scored higher over the three days of racing, the two clubs had previously agreed that each day's racing would be scored separately, so Beverly YC won by scoring better on two of the race days.

The Knockabout class didn't fare as well as the Raceabouts. Club members derided them as "leakabouts," so in 1902 the club promoted a design competition in *Forest & Stream* to replace them, offering prizes of $100, $50, and $25 for the best three entries. Despite receiving more than 50 entries, the club was not satisfied, feeling the proposed designs were not sufficiently powerful. They turned to club member Crane, who produced a 24-foot-overall keelboat that was 15 feet on the waterline. The boat carried 350 square feet of sail on a 6-foot beam, with the keel drawing 3 feet, 9 inches. The delivered price of the boats, built by the S. Ayers yard in Nyack, New York, was $632.25 apiece ($12,600 today). The club ordered 17 immediately, upping the fleet to 24 by the start of the spring season.

Although designed for racing, many owners of Herreshoff S-class sloops treat them as very well-designed coastal cruisers, like these sailors enjoying a sail near Eggemogin Reach.

Alison Langley

The boats looked very much like the Herreshoff 15-footer, and were, by all reports, both fast and wet. Crane took his first test sail of his new boat in December 1902, in a fresh breeze with a temperature of 8 degrees Fahrenheit. Although it was no doubt a short, cold outing, Crane reported that "she handled beautifully."

The Seawanhaka Corinthian YC racing fleet consisted primarily of men, as was the fashion in those days, but it is notable that there was also the "Ladies Race." In the early years the women competed in the 15-footers. The results for the Ladies Race were listed alongside the men's results, but the concept of mixing the sexes in a single boat was still in the future.

A significant change in the philosophy of award selection came about in 1912. The established practice had been to scale the size of the trophy to the size of the boat, regardless of the number of competitors. This didn't set well with many members, presumably those who sailed the smaller boats. They took offense that, in some cases, winners from the larger boat classes were given credits at local jewelers with instructions to choose their prize and have it engraved in a manner the winner felt appropriate.

The Trustees and Race Committee of the Seawanhaka Corinthian YC decided to begin awarding trophies of no special value—attractive, yes, but not scaled

to the size of the boat; rather, the trophies reflected the value of the race or event. This new practice was evidently popular, as other clubs soon emulated it.

Another change for the period involved the Ladies Races, which moved from the 15-footer class to another, newer class; the Nut.

The first season for the Nut class, designed by Cox & Stevens, was 1915. These spirited boats, just 22 feet overall, suited the ideals of the Seawanhaka Corinthian YC perfectly, as the first fleet of 24 boats was built for just $99 each ($1,700 today). The trustees of the Seawanhaka Corinthian YC voted to reduce hauling and storage fees for the new class from $10 to $7.50.

The boats, featuring low freeboard, a sliding gunter rig, a squared-off punt bow, and a dagger board, carried 173 square feet of sail, and capsized so frequently they earned the nickname the "Suicide Class." Suicidal or not, they were immediately popular, and early on all of the boats were named, of course, after some sort of nut. There was *Cocoanut* [sic], *Filbert*, *Brazil Nut*, and so on; the one exception was *Josephus*, owned by Colgate Hoyt Jr., brother of Sherman Hoyt.

The naming of this boat was a subtle dig at the expense of Josephus Daniels, secretary of the U.S. Navy from 1913 to 1921. Daniels was the man who forever stopped the consumption of alcohol aboard U.S. naval vessels, and he is the reason people talk of a "cup of Joe" in reference to coffee; the phrase began among sailors who had to get used to coffee rather than the beer and wine they had been drinking prior to Daniels' tenure as naval secretary.

Daniels didn't take kindly to this—Sherman Hoyt later had difficulty obtaining an officer's commission in the U.S. Navy; meanwhile, the Nut class remained popular with Seawanhaka Corinthian YC members. It wasn't

until the appearance of the Herreshoff Fish class that the Nut's numbers began to decline.

The first mention of this famous class was in the minutes of a Seawanhaka Corinthian YC trustees' meeting in 1914, where they decided upon the Herreshoff design. A brief financial depression slowed the purchase of these boats, which at $1,000 apiece were much more expensive than the popular Nut boats. It wasn't until the winter of 1915–1916 that any were built.

Finally, by spring of 1916, 18 of the 21-foot-overall boats were built, carrying 1,200 pounds of outside ballast pushed along by 262 square feet of sail distributed in gaff mainsail and a clubfooted jib. As an omen of things to come, they also carried what was for the time a proportionate spinnaker, although the 'chute, by today's standards, was quite modest. In pleasant contrast to the Nut, the Fish class was fairly stable, and, in another portent, there was a watertight bulkhead forward of the mast.

The boat was an immediate success. The club again reduced the storage and hauling fees, holding charges to

A close look at the cockpit of the S-boat shows some very modern thinking for a 1920 boat. All lines lead to the coachroof, including the mainsheet, on the large center winch. Running backstays allow a long boom and a lot of roach. *Alison Langley*

Seawanhaka Corinthian YC member Clifton Crane designed the 12-meter *Gleam*, sail number 11, in 1937, and Olin Stephens designed *Northern Light* in 1938. *Northern Light* was a gift from Lee Loomis Sr. to his son Lee Jr. as an enticement to keep him from going to Europe in 1938. *Paul Darling*

just $20 to haul, store, and relaunch the boats. Period race results show that the women took to the boat as well, with the Ladies Race results noting they raced more Fish-class boats than Nuts.

During the years of World War I, sailing as a sport was much reduced everywhere in the country. By 1920, however, the boom was on, and the Fish class dominated weekend club racing. The bigger classes, the New York 30s and 40s, were still raced, but their days were numbered.

The big news of 1920 was the introduction of another Herreshoff, the beloved S–class. The boat had

been designed the year before, with a full bow and stern and, for the time, rather short overhangs. Measuring 27 feet, 6 inches overall, the waterline length was 20 feet, 6 inches, with a period-perfect 7-foot beam. Most notably, the S-class came rigged with the new bermudan main, termed at the time a "Marconi rig" because of the perceived resemblance of the mast to a radio transmitting tower (Guglielmo Marconi being the inventor of radio). As with the Stars' first bermudan rigs, the early S-class boats carried a curved mast— expensive to make but thought to improve the set of the new fangled triangular main.

The Seawanhaka Corinthian YC began racing S-class boats regularly in 1922, with 15 races that year.

The S-class boats became very popular, with clubs along the length of the East Coast buying fleets. Eventually, upward of 150 of the boats were built, a remarkable number for a boat that at $2,000 apiece ($20,000 today) was twice the price of a Fish-class model. S-class boats are still popular today, and their value has appreciated nicely over the years.

Meanwhile, the Seawanhaka Cup was once again truly an international competition. In 1926, the club's trustees changed the Declaration of Trust back to its original form, ruling out any challenges originating from the United States. Thereafter, challenges for the Cup would have to come from a country other than that which held the trophy, restoring it as a truly international challenge. Much of the racing took place in 6-meter boats, although the 1929 series was raced in 8-meters. Even though many of the competing boats were built in the United States, the 6-meter design is not, strictly speaking, an American one.

In 1925, sailors in the New York area began asking for a boat to fit between the Star boats and the 6-meter boats. The effort to fill the need was led by members of the Seawanhaka Corinthian YC, chiefly Carroll Alker. The boat was to cost less than a 6-meter, be suitable for junior sailors, and be a comfortable daysailer.

The club put out a request for designs, selecting one by Charles D. Mower, a New York City naval architect. Although the Seawanhaka Corinthian YC instigated the design search, a number of clubs in the area were involved, so the name selected for the new design was the Sound Interclub.

The yard chosen to build the first fleet of 28 was the Harry B. Nevins yard of City Island, New York. Those first boats came in at the affordable price of $2,400 ($23,000), which included a set of Ratsey sails. As a testimonial to the design's success in meeting the requirement that it be suitable for junior sailors, several of the boats were bought for use by children, both boys and girls. Although the design had no head, some of the first boats had added, at slight additional cost, small heads installed under the cabin transom, making the boat a proper pocket cruiser.

That first fleet of Sound Interclubs was raced in clubs all over the Long Island Sound area, with a total of nine different clubs represented. Only four of the boats raced came from the Seawanhaka Corinthian YC. The first

The Shields class, designed by Olin Stephens, has an extremely high ballast ratio of over 60 percent and a class rule that allows only one set of sails per season. *Rosenfeld collection, Mystic, Connecticut*

boats were thought to be a bit underballasted, as the designer thought the specified crew of four would provide the necessary ballast to get the boat down on its designed waterline and enable it to stand up to weather. Less than a month after the first boats were launched, additional lead was added in the form of two slabs inserted in keel deadwood above the existing ballast. This further stiffened the boat and allowed an increase in sail area, accomplished with a larger main, extending the full length of the boom, and the addition of 18 inches to the hoist of the jib, increasing its area by roughly 3 square feet.

To keep the sport of sailing alive and growing, the Seawanhaka Corinthian YC realized that it needed to include as many family members as possible. The children of adult sailors were taken on board as "bilge boys" or used smaller-class boats in junior racing programs. The Seawanhaka Corinthian YC also had an embryonic junior program as early as the beginning of the twentieth century. Things really changed in 1936, when the Seawanhaka Corinthian YC organized the Seawanhaka Corinthian Junior Yacht Club. A separate clubhouse for the junior sailors, under consideration by club members for at least two years previous, was finally built that year and dedicated during the club's Fourth of July festivities.

By 1937, the Junior Club had 137 members. They raced Seabirds, a 24-foot-overall keel sloop designed by Olin Stephens. A fleet of 29 boats raced the year of the class' introduction, and the post of Junior Instructor became a paid position within the club. So seriously was the junior program taken that the Seawanhaka Corinthian YC provided what was termed the Junior Launch, the *Emerald*, to cruise to various points in the club area to pick up children for the day's instruction.

Emerald was one of a pair of vessels, the other one being *Resolute*, that were used as club launches. Designed

by Nat Herreshoff for the U.S. Navy as a captain's gig, Herreshoff refused to sell the lines to the Navy because he didn't want to build more of them at his yard. *Resolute* became the tender for the 1920 America's Cup defender of the same name, and the Seawanhaka Corinthian YC bought it in 1921.

Within the junior club, boys and girls were seen in near-equal numbers. In 1939, a crew of young girls was taken aboard the 72-foot-overall yawl-rigged ocean racer, *Baruna*, for an overnight sail. While Junior racers had their own events in such boats as the Seabird, there were regular events called the Junior Cruise, in which large boats, such as the 12-meters *Gleam, Seven Seas,* and *Northern Light,* and New York 32s such as *Rampage, Notus,* and *Clotho,* took Junior sailors out for a taste of sailing "real" boats.

For most of the years of American involvement in World War II, racing did not take place. In 1942, a few small races were held, but full racing did not resume until 1945.

In 1950, Seawanhaka Corinthian YC members introduced the Raven, a 24-foot-overall centerboard planing sloop that soon became a national class. The U.S. Coast Guard Academy was the first customer for this boat, which Roger McAleer designed to carry a racing crew of three. The boat was originally built of molded plywood, but the class organization got on the fiberglass bandwagon in 1951.

Many of the boats that club members raced in the post–World War II era were popular in their own right. Even the Shields, a product of club member Cornelius Shields' inspiration, was sailed more outside the club than within it. These boats, on which Seawanhaka Corinthian YC members won many national championships, included the Soling and the Etchells 22, designed by E. W. Etchells to be the next Olympic boat. To his dismay, the Soling, designed by Norwegian Jan Herman Linge, became the Olympic keelboat.

For the first seven decades of the twentieth century, the Seawanhaka Corinthian YC played a pivotal role in the development of the American sailboat, nurturing one-design construction and class racing. As the sport developed, however, manufacturers, rather than clubs, often introduced new designs in the hope of producing

the next big class. Clubs such as the Seawanhaka Corinthian had no such pecuniary goals; they simply wanted boats that sailed well and were affordable for their members. Many of the boats that came from that philosophy are still sailed today. ✳

J. B. Dunbaugh, vice-commodore of the Larchmont YC, owned this Sound Interclub, *Aileen*. Close-hauled during an early race, it sports a single headsail, although an inner staysail was part of the sail plan. Cornelius Shields usually sailed *Aileen*. Considered the premier small-boat sailor of Long Island Sound, Shields conceptualized the Olin Stephens one-design in 1962. *Aileen* was predicted to be the class champ in the class' inaugural year. It eventually finished second in the Long Island Sound Yacht Racing Association's 1926 series, behind *Wee Betty*, owned by G. M. L. LaBranche of the Larchmont YC and sailed by Bill Swain. *Rosenfeld collection, Mystic, Connecticut*

For Business and Pleasure

East Coast Sailboats

For the great majority of sailors, their activities on the water were unsung and unheralded. They weren't members of a yacht club; their "club" was an impromptu gathering on the pier after a day's sail, and they didn't follow rules, handicaps, or any design principle other than "if it looks right it is right."

There was, nonetheless, a certain similarity to many of their boats, as most of them traced their design roots to work boats, vessels designed for their utilitarian functions rather than for going faster than another sailor's boat.

Speed, of course, always played a role, as it does in any sailboat. Sailors will tell you that all it takes for a race is to have two sailboats on the same tack, and they're right, whether they are yachts or working sailboats. The sailors of working boats didn't want to spend any more time on the water than necessary, not out of any inherent dislike of the environment but rather because the longer one was out, the greater the exposure to weather, the longer one had to store the catch, and, perhaps most importantly the first boats back had the choice of market and usually better prices.

The boats of the United States' East Coast, in many cases, were of the working–boat mold. All along this coast, sailing was a way of life. Beset by tides, currents, fog, rocks, and with few

Friendship sloops, blessed with a name that reveals both their place of origin and what any owner will tell you is the

nature of the vessel, are a near-perfect example of the transformation of work boat to pleasure boat. *Alison Langley*

sheltered harbors, sailboats developed as rugged, seaworthy vessels, a cherished part of the coastal environment and economy.

An excellent early example is the Muscongus boat, used by Maine lobstermen to set and retrieve lobster traps. It eventually became popular with people whose only exposure to lobster was on a plate. Graceful, with a swooping sheer, a wide beam, and a sharp turn to the bilge, the Muscongus sloop is now most well known in its evolved state as the Friendship sloop, which Wilbur Morse built and designed in Friendship, Maine.

The Friendship sloop nearly disappeared as oystermen put engines into boats that were designed as motorboats; their salvation was their seakindly manner, as well as their wonderful good looks. Instead of disappearing from the scene, the Friendship sloop was embraced as a pleasure boat both by Maine residents and people who had summer houses along the Maine coast.

Working Friendships, and thus Friendships built for pleasure, varied in length from 21 to 50 feet, but there was a set of proportional "rules" that were applied when building the boat, or sometimes even drawing one for construction.

They all had a graceful elliptical stern, for example, and at the other end a clipper bow supported a bowsprit. The beam measured one-third the length, and the height of the mast equaled the length overall plus half the draft. These formulae kept the boats recognizable, regardless of size, although calling them a one-design is a bit of a stretch.

The first Friendships were, of course, built of wood, but it wasn't long before fiberglass was introduced, a step met with some trepidation by the more traditional owners, but one that ensured the survival of the boat for the enjoyment of future generations of sailors and admirers.

As more Friendships were built for pleasure sailing, the number of owners grew to the point that an owners' association became inevitable. It wasn't until 1961, however, when 14 of the graceful boats gathered for a regatta and races in Friendship, Maine, that the Friendship Sloop

Society was born. Now, the regatta is held annually in July, still off the coast of the sloop's namesake hometown.

On the Chesapeake, as with most of the other sailing areas, work boats established the design of boats that were eventually used for pleasure, and some of the handsomest and most well known evolved from the bugeye and the skipjack.

The line of evolution began with the log canoe, a centerboard boat built of logs, pinned together to form the hull. Some of the boats had two sets of sails: a "working" set, small enough to handle with a load of oysters, and another, larger set of racing sails.

Log canoe races began as entertainment for the watermen, who would bet on their favorite and race on the local rivers, including the Chester, the Miles, and the Tred Avon. The racing scene with log canoes slowly disappeared among the working watermen around the beginning of the twentieth century, but wealthy yachtsmen adopted the boat in the 1930s, commissioning log canoes built for racing.

The well-off sailors who had the boats built neither needed nor bought "working" sails. These boats were built for racing, and the more sail that could be laced onto the masts, the faster the boat would go. Lacking any external ballast, the crews resorted to springboards in an effort to keep the boats upright. These were long planks, at first one and later several, that the crew extended to windward and sat upon. This created a tricky calculus of balance, with the crew perilously perched 8 or 10 feet out over the water, lined up, and

Friendship sloops continue to be made. The 31-foot Friendship *Liberty*, built in 1980 at the Newman yard on Cranberry Island, Maine, is traditionally rigged, with deadeyes and a laced-on main, but the skipper had better tend to that anchor soon. *Alison Langley*

44

sitting in a row. Moving inboard in response to a lull in the wind was of necessity rather slow, and it was equally laborious to move out. Crews often found themselves in the water, whether from being dropped to windward or catapulted to leeward.

They were fast, though; a skilled helmsman and a nimble crew could keep the boats flying in winds that would capsize any other boat with a similar sail area-to-displacement ratio. Racing became serious business, and boats were commissioned especially for racing, thus renewing a

The 35-foot log canoe *Flying Cloud*, built in 1932, was commissioned as a racing boat. A five-log canoe, it was built by John Harrison, who also built *Jay Dee*. Winner of the Governor's Cup in 1934, its rig was reduced in the 1940s and the boat became a cruiser, but in 1975, it began to race again. Note the slack sheets on the mizzen; keeping these boats upright is a constant balancing act, literally, between power and the crew's windward position.

Marc Castelli

craft that nearly died out in the years from the beginning of the twentieth century until 1933, when the John B. Harrison yard was commissioned to build the *Jay Dee* and the *Flying Cloud*. Harrison, it should be mentioned, was also the builder of the *Edna B. Lockwood*, and the name Harrison—both the yard and Harrison himself—was well known in the boatbuilding and racing world. Harrison was a hard-driving skipper who, in response to his crew's asking him to reef during a race, replied that he would rather "let the wind blow them off."

From the log canoe evolved a number of vessels for cargo or oyster-dredging work, all distinguished by what might be seen as very generous sail areas. The brogan was made from hollowed-out logs—five, seven, and, later, nine logs—just as was the log canoe. As the boat developed, freeboard and load-carrying were increased by adding boards to the top layer of logs. From the brogan came the bugeye and, inevitably, competition

sorted out the faster boats, as the oystermen raced back to port to get the first, and best, prices.

Some of these boats survive to the present day, such as the *Edna B. Lockwood*, still carving the waters around the Chesapeake Bay Maritime Museum in St. Michael's, Maryland. The *Edna B.* was a working bugeye from 1888, when it was launched, until 1967, when it was purchased and then donated to the museum, which rebuilt the bugeye in a project that resulted in virtually a new boat. Relaunched in 1979, the *Edna B.* now sails and races on a regular basis.

The ketch-rigged, centerboard bugeyes carried a large headsail, with a gaff mainsail and foresail. The main and foremast were steeply raked, as much as 15 degrees, allowing the use of halyards for cargo hoisting and eliminating the need for backstays. This configuration permitted a longer boom and larger sails, and they had a well-deserved reputation for speed. The hull, usually double-ended, was finely proportioned, although there were a few round-sterned bugeyes built as well, possibly to increase the usable cargo capacity.

There were two basic varieties of bugeyes, "chunk" boats and "frame" boats. The earlier bugeyes were chunk boats, built from log sections as were their predecessors, the log canoes. This made for very thick hull sections, at least 8 to 10 inches on the bottom, tapering somewhat toward the gunwales, where there were planks fitted to raise the freeboard. Frame bugeyes were built of planks, resembling the chunk boats in shape but much lighter

and capable of carrying more cargo. They were superior in most respects because of this, and by the end of the nineteenth century, most bugeyes were frame-built.

Despite this seeming uniformity of construction methods, bugeyes, most of them around 50–60 feet in length, weren't built in accordance with any certain "rules." The builders used the methods that were most familiar and that worked. Bugeyes usually began as nothing more than half-models, and while no two were identical, they were sufficiently recognizable as bugeyes. Their similarities were driven by function: what worked

The bugeye *Edna B. Lockwood* was built at the Harrison yard. To conform with oystering regulations, bugeyes were built without engines, and they are the last of the working sail in the United States. *Marc Castelli*

(*previous page*) The skipjack, last of America's working sail, still drags for oysters in Chesapeake Bay, heading out in the evening light for a night's work. The 40-foot *Hilda* M. *Willing*, built in 1905, hails from Tilghman Island, Maryland. *Starke Jett*

The pungy yacht *Kessie* C. *Price* was built in 1888 at Rock Creek, on Deal's Island, Maryland. *Kessie*, 55 feet long, has an 18-foot, 7-inch beam, draws 5 feet with the board up, and is classified as a "she" pungy, so-called because it has a centerboard as well as a keel. *Chesapeake Bay Maritime Museum*

in earlier boats was continued, and those traits found not to contribute to their efficiency as work boats were discarded.

The bugeye's ketch rig had a huge mizzen, practically schooner-sized—indeed, the bugeye was sometimes classed as a schooner—and its ability in going to windward was widely praised. This was attributed to the steep rake of the masts, in accordance with the so-called "lift line" theory.

According to this theory, greater drive can be expected from a sail that is designed or arranged on the mast so that an imaginary line connecting the centers of lift of the sails is vertical rather than canted forward, as would happen with a mast that was vertical. No less a critic than L. Frances Herreshoff lent credence to this theory in a letter to Robert Johnson in 1966, in which he wrote that, "It has been the common knowledge of sailor men for centuries that a lifting sail (as they used to call it) is much more efficient than a depressing sail."

Be that as it may, there is little evidence of this effect in the more technical literature on the subject, and some of the bugeye's speed may instead be attributed to the increased sail area allowed by the lack of a backstay. A more easily determined result of the mast rake is that the center of effort of the sail remains essentially the same as the sail is reefed down, thus reducing the onset of weather helm.

Skipjacks were the next step in the evolution of the oyster working boat, and also descended from the log canoe. While there were boats called skipjacks in use in the Gulf of Mexico in the years before the turn of the twentieth century, it was on the Chesapeake Bay that the boat and its type truly matured. Made of planks rather than logs, it went together quicker than log-built

boats and provided more room for the oyster payload. The low deadrise of the log canoe was recognizable, but the aft section soon developed a V-shaped deadrise, giving more lateral stability, making boats with this design more maneuverable as well. The centerboard allowed for balancing the center of lateral resistance, useful when trying to maintain the vessel under way with the load of dragging nets.

The speed of the boat when dredging was critical. At less than 2 knots, the dredge would dig into the bottom, stopping the boat. More than 3 or 4 knots and the dredge would skip over the bottom, missing the oysters. The ability to reduce or add to effective sail area, sometimes by merely slacking the sheets, made this a good working boat, and later, when being raced, aided in keeping the boat right side up during one of the Bay's notorious puffs or squalls.

The skipjack carried a single mast, raked well aft in the manner that was becoming increasingly used at the time, with a boom that extended beyond the transom. The fractional jib, often with a boom but always self-tacking, was also large.

Perhaps the handsomest of the Bay working boats that metamorphosed into yachts was the pungy, which was used for both oystering and cargo carrying. Schooner-rigged, pungies had all the "right" lines for attracting the eye, with a swooping, low freeboard that promised water-scooping lee rails on a reach, a graceful clipper bow, and a massive amount of sail, including a large headsail that gave the vessel enough power, when added to the two large gaff sails, to pull two oyster dredges to windward. From a distance, a pungy with all sails set would bring to mind the Baltimore clipper, with whom the pungy shared a fair amount of genetic material.

Pungies were known for speed. They were often larger than bugeyes, and came in two varieties: the standard pungy, with a vestigial keel, and the "she" pungy, with a centerboard in addition to the keel.

In the realm of smaller boats, the Comet class is, at least technically speaking, a Chesapeake Bay boat, designed by C. Lowndes Johnson, who lived in Miles

Showing the wonderful mix of boats on the Chesapeake, a Comet works to leeward of a log canoe, with a fleet of Penguins to starboard, on the Mills River. *Chesapeake Bay Maritime Museum*

River, near Easton, Maryland, on the Chesapeake Bay. Johnson won the Star Internationals in 1929, in company with his brother Graham, and was known as both a designer and builder, especially of Star-class boats.

In 1932, he designed a 16-foot centerboard dinghy in response to a request from Mrs. Elliot Wheel, a resident of Easton, Maryland. She wanted what has become almost the standard request from people seeking a one-design dinghy. It had to be inexpensive to own, easy to build, and easy to handle. It also had to be sufficiently exciting on the water to provide good competition for her sons, who wanted to compete in the handicap races held regularly at nearby Oxford.

Johnson, who admired the lines of the Star, drew what became thought of as a Star boat without the keel. They weren't called Comets right away; those first boats were known as Crabs, and the plans, published in *Yachting* in March 1932, were an immediate success.

It wasn't until 1933 that the Comets took off, when John Eiman and Wilbur Haines, two doctors with a penchant for sailing, went looking for a small, inexpensive one-design boat at the New York Motor Boat Show. The Great Depression was hitting everyone, it seems, and smaller boats were attracting a lot more attention.

The boat had had a name change; *Yachting* magazine was calling it the "Star Junior," because of its resemblance to the hard-chine keelboat that was so popular. The doctors were from Stone Harbor, New Jersey, and they wanted the boat for their club. When they saw the boat, they remembered having seen it racing during a visit to Oxford, Maryland, and were impressed with its performance, so they decided that this was their boat.

Learning from the Star, which became so popular in part because of its well-organized, almost aggressive, class organization, the men and some of the first owners met at *Yachting*'s offices in New York. One of the first orders of business was a name change. The final choice, Comet, harkened back to its design influence

and gave the boat a name they felt was perfectly descriptive of its character.

The Comet was a success. It planed, one of the first of the small-planing dinghies, and carried a spinnaker that further enhanced its downwind performance. The 300-pound boat, drawing 3 feet with the board down, has attracted some very serious sailors. Among the more well known of the national champions were "Bus" Mosbacher, who skippered *Weatherly* in the 1962 America's Cup contest, and U.S. Olympic Sailing Team members Andy Schoettle and Harry Sindle.

Another design that endeared itself to sailors on the Bay and elsewhere, from the waning years of World War II to the early 1960s, was the Owens Cutter, a 40-foot, 6-inch boat with graceful overhangs that kept the waterline to 28 feet. The boat was the product of the

Owens Yacht Company, in Baltimore, Maryland. The Owens yard was well known for its powerboats, but this seems to have been an economic decision, as the three Owens brothers were known as enthusiastic sailors, especially Norman, who actively campaigned a New York 32 during the war years. He liked the boat's light displacement, and this influenced his design of the Owens Cutter.

Norman explained that the boat resembled a New York 32 in its displacement and midbody section, and that the 30-square-meter boats had inspired the aft sections. What made the boat unique, though, in those years before fiberglass production, were the assembly-line methods used in its construction.

The first five boats were built conventionally at the M. M. Davis yard, of Solomons Island, Maryland. After that, building was taken over by the Owens yard, where the boats were assembled from pre-made parts and built upside down, from the deck up, using what Owens called the "Duraform" method.

A steel jig placed each of the roughly 3,500 parts in its proper place. Separate jigs were used for the keel, the cabin, the cockpit, and so on. This method allowed assembly-line methods to be applied to what were still hand-built wooden boats, and the yard turned them out in what were, for the boat's size, relatively large numbers. The first Owens Cutter, called *Den-E-Von*, was sailed to Florida in 1946 and won the St. Petersburg–Havana Race. This victory inspired other buyers; by the end of the 1940s, the Owens yard had produced 41 of the fast boats.

Their good looks were as much a factor in their commercial success as their speed. The Owens Cutter had a freeboard that would not be at all out of place on a contemporary boat, although for its time it was somewhat high. This did much to keep the crews dry in the offshore racing circuit, and opened the eyes of buyers to designs that maintained good looks while incorporating design factors that aided in comfort. The cabin trunk,

The Owens Cutter *Snallygaster*, shown here during the 1967 Block Island Race, was a successful racer as were most of the other Owens Cutters. The earlier, lighter Owens-built boats were reputed to be faster than the later Hinckley boats. *Rosenfeld collection, Mystic, Connecticut*

The Comet shows what some see as its Lightning heritage as it heels, with the hard chines providing additional lateral resistance. *Rosenfeld collection, Mystic, Connecticut*

nestled in that high freeboard, was attractively low, and the overhangs, well balanced in profile, contributed to a longer waterline when heeled, the freeboard keeping the lee rail from causing drag by being pulled along under invading waves.

Around 1950, just 10 years before the end of the Owens yard, the Henry R. Hinckley Company took over production, modifying the boat by adding half a ton of ballast and increasing the sail area. The Hinckley yard began to make the boat in fiberglass, and then, in the sort of evolution so common with boat design, the Owens Cutter morphed into the Hinckley 41, after undergoing changes in the hull and appendages.

On the New Jersey coast, in Barnegat Bay, a small boat called the sneakbox evolved from diminutive, one-person boats used for shooting waterfowl and other activities that aren't always associated with the gentlemanly sport of sailing. As with other utilitarian watercraft, though, the sneakbox was soon adopted by sailors for swifter-moving recreational purposes. The boats came with a fine pedigree. Their length varied, from 12 to 20 feet, and they were, in their early days, almost entirely owner-built. They were decked over, with a small cockpit reminiscent of that of a kayak. They were low, almost scowlike, and the early hunting models drew very little water with the board up: literally a few inches of water would float one. With the board down, draft was around 2 feet. They were rowed or sailed, and rowlocks were often included even when the boats became racing sailboats.

The sneakbox was extremely versatile, making documented voyages from New York to Miami and the length of the Mississippi River. Sometimes small runners were built on the hull, allowing the boat to be used on ice. The deck plan definitely resembled a scow, with a bow overhang of a foot or so, and a plum, flat transom. Early sneakboxes were either spritsail or gaff-rigged, but

the bermudan rig was adopted, in 1924, about the same time as its use became widespread in the Star class.

Around 1906, sailors involved in racing sneakboxes formulated class rules. They were at first very loosely structured. The boats could be no longer than 20 feet, but virtually everything else was left to the builder and the sailor. Sail area ranged from 450 to 600 square feet, with a gaff main. The mast was stepped very far forward—a sneakbox could have passed for a catboat. Later sneakboxes had a small jib, and eventually a bowsprit was added, increasing the jib area and materially improving the handling.

With the formation of class rules, sneakboxes left the realm of working boat and became pleasure boats. The great latitude afforded by the rules made for some interesting boats, and by 1910 some 50 boats had been built. They carried sandbags for movable ballast, and contemporary reports tell of racing crews of six or eight, carrying as many as 35 bags of sand, each weighing some 30 pounds, and each needing to be moved during a tack. The bags were made for the boat, sewn closed and with a rope handle facilitating their movement. These early racing sneakboxes carried a large rudder, generated tremendous weather helm when they were pushed hard, and in a tacking duel, the winner was likely to be determined more by the physical prowess of the crew than sailing skill.

Probably due in part to the difficulties of racing these boats, by 1914 a new fleet, to a revised design, was launched by two local yacht clubs: the Island Heights Yacht Club and the Sea Side Park Yacht Club. Charles D. Mower designed them all, and this was pretty much the end of the builder-designed boats. No longer were the boats stuffed with sandbags and weightlifters. The gaff sails were much smaller, the boats were lighter, and the transom-hung rudder was also smaller. The changes were well received, as the boats handled better and sailed faster. In a short time even the diehards with their sandbags were convinced.

The 20-footers were so popular that, in 1918, a class of 15-footers was introduced. The class was formally organized in 1920, when the Polyhue Yacht Club purchased a fleet of seven boats. The Perrine sneakboxes, as they were known, were named after J. H. Perrine, who originated the class and from whom the first fleet was purchased. In keeping with the club's name, the sails were all of different colors. The Polyhue YC fell from sight in 1933, another victim of the Great Depression, and its clubhouse became the local community center. In 1939, the club reorganized as the Beachwood Yacht Club, of Beachwood, New Jersey.

In 1922 the Barnegat Bay Yacht Racing Association recognized the Perrine sneakbox as a class, and by then fleets of 40 boats on the starting line were not unusual. As with many other classes, early rules were fairly loose, but in the course of competition and sailors doing what they could to increase performance, the Perrine sneakbox class rules began to define everything from bottom paint to ballast.

By 1923, it became apparent that crew weight was a factor that needed some regulation, and so the Barnegat Bay Yacht Racing Association divided the Perrine sneakbox fleet into classes, A and B, determined by two factors: the age of the skipper and crew, and the weight of the sail. Class B, the "junior" class, specified 6-ounce cotton sails and a crew no older than 17 at the start of the season. Class A allowed 4-1/2-ounce sails and had no age restrictions. Sail area was the same for both classes, at 165 square feet, a far cry from those early sandbag sneakboxes carrying four times the sail area.

The Perrine sneakboxes had a more conventional-looking bow, without the bluff, scowlike deck plan of the 20-footers and the earlier Barnegat Bay sneakboxes. From the centerboard slot aft, a small skeg ran all the way to the transom, and there was a coaming surrounding the cockpit, which had rudimentary slat-type seats on both sides.

Two variations were raced. The early versions carried a gaff main, cat-rigged with a forestay, while later boats had a clubfooted jib on a short bowsprit and a bermudan main. The boats were standardized at 15 feet overall, and 13 feet on the waterline, drawing 6 inches with the board up. They had a barn-door rudder, reminiscent of that on a catboat, and with their 5-foot, 9-inch beam and an all-up weight of 400 pounds, provided comfortable, safe sailing for junior club members. They were very affordable, as well—one of the necessities for a boat bought by the fleet by yacht clubs and designed for use by youngsters. The price, in the years around 1925, was $225, which translates into about $2,200 in today's money.

The smaller boats were affordable and widely enjoyed, but there is nothing that says "American sailboat" more than the schooner. The first schooners that were sailing as yachts along the East Coast were converted from Gloucester fishing boats, built tough and fast to work the Grand Banks. When fishing boats began to carry ice aboard and delivered fresh (rather than salted) fish to the docks, speed became imperative. Once the hold was filled with iced-down fish, every hour's delay in selling the fish meant a loss in quality.

The schooner rig, with its sail area divided up among several smaller sails, suited shorthanded crews admirably, and the boat had a reputation for speed. With the end of World War I, sailors were ready to cast off the austerity of the war years and get back on the water. John Alden's designs appealed to people who wanted a family cruising yacht, without the necessity of hiring a professional crew.

The growth of offshore sailing contributed to the popularity of schooners, as they were more suitable for cruising and racing of soundings than the lightly rigged coastal vessels. Alden's schooners came almost directly from working fishing schooners, and were well proven.

The average sailor's horizons began to broaden helped by Wilhelm II, emperor of Germany, who inspired a transatlantic race in 1905. He put up a solid-gold cup, to be awarded to the fastest boat to cover a course beginning off Sandy Hook, New Jersey, and finishing off "the Lizard" peninsula, on the southwestern tip of England.

Rogue, one of Nathanael Herreshoff's Newport 29s, has an excellent pedigree. In the opinion of many sailors, the Newport 29 is Nat Herreshoff's best all-round design. *Paul Darling*

Eleven boats entered, and, putting to rest the skeptics, they all finished, but none in the spectacular fashion of the William Gardner–designed schooner *Atlantic*. Driven hard and fast by a professional skipper, Charley Barr, *Atlantic* set a record for the crossing that stood for nearly 100 years—12 days, four hours, and one minute.

Barr was the right man for the job: he had successfully defended the America's Cup three times and was known as a skipper who saw taking in a reef as being tantamount to losing.

The Kaiser's Cup Race, as it was called, was the first major ocean race for American yachting. There were two earlier match races held in the waning years of the nineteenth century, but this event started a trend and set the format for future races. Popular magazines covering such events helped change sailors' views of offshore sailing, especially articles by Thomas Fleming Day, the editor of *The Rudder*.

Day's work to popularize ocean racing began in 1904, with a race from Brooklyn, New York, to Marblehead, Massachusetts, a distance of some 330 miles. In keeping with Day's philosophy, the race consisted of small boats, with the largest of the six-strong fleet measuring less than 30 feet on the waterline.

Day wrote in *The Rudder* that he could not "praise too highly the courage and skill of all those who engaged in the race . . . I have been doing it for years. But it was different with the other yacht crews. . . . all praise to you, boys! It made my old heart glad. . . ."

He followed that race with another in 1905, from Brooklyn to Hampton Roads, Virginia. This race, which occurred a few months after the Kaiser's Cup, was certainly inspired by that event. Newspapers of the time were vocal in their criticism of ocean racing, stating that small boats had no business offshore and that the sailors were tempting fate, if not survival. This was a red flag to Day, who didn't need much to set him off. In *The Rudder* he took the newspaper writers to task, saying their information had been gathered by talking with "a lot of gray-headed rum-soaked piazza scows . . . miserable old hulks who spend their days swigging booze on the front stoop of a clubhouse . . . what does the average yachtsman know about sea sailing? Absolutely nothing! Then let him hold his tongue."

Day's badinage was slow to pay off, but he had truly started something. In 1906, he organized the first Bermuda Race, and only three boats entered, despite the publicity engendered by the Kaiser's Cup the year before. In 1907, there were 12 entries, and in 1910, when there were only two starters (one of whom was John Alden), the race seemed moribund and wasn't held again until 1923. Day's faith in the phenomenon of ocean racing was eventually vindicated; in 1923, after a 13-year hiatus, 22 boats entered the Bermuda Race, 17 of which were schooners.

The winner of this race was *Malabar IV*, designed and owned by Alden. Alden picked the name after seeing it on old charts of Cape Cod. (The cape has long since eroded away, and what was once the point called Malabar is now Bearse Shoal.) Alden designated the various *Malabars* (13

are known, although Alden's records evidence a *Malabar XV*, designated Design Number 901A; nothing is known of a *Malabar XIV*) with admitted influence from the working boats of Gloucester. Alden wrote in a magazine article in 1928 that "the first of my *Malabars* has the fisherman as the basis of its design . . . Let us look at the true fisherman as exemplified in the Gloucesterman, which I have always admired."

The Alden office worked with a tightly knit group of draftsmen and designers, and some notable boats came from the drawing boards of those working there. Carl Alberg, for example, drew the lines for *Malabar XI*, the first of the yawl- or ketch-rigged *Malabars*.

There is some design affinity between the Alden schooners and the Friendship sloops. Alden is said to have admired the boat's lines, and openly expressed admiration for the Morse schooner, *Lloyd W. Berry*.

Paid crews had fallen from favor with the moneyed crowd, and were not an option for sailors of more ordinary means. Accordingly, Alden, as well as other designers, began to draw boats that could be sailed by a small, amateur crew. Alden said that he "wanted a cruising

The brogan was the next boat in the evolution from the bugeye to the skipjack, and the similarities are apparent. *Mustang*, built in 1907 in Saxis, Virginia, and launched as the *Kate D.*, is on the national historic registry. *Chesapeake Bay Maritime Museum*

(*opposite*) The Manhasset One-Design, which began life as the Sound Junior Class, was designed by Olin Stephens in 1929, and has the distinction of being S&S Design Number 1. Its name was changed after World War II. Commissioned by the Junior Yacht Racing Association of Long Island Sound, it is 21 feet, 6 inches overall, and 15 feet on the waterline. Of the boats, Stephens has said, "the shape and proportions seem appropriate to the size." *Alison Langley*

boat in which I could go anywhere along shore or off the coast, that would stay at sea in almost any weather, and at the same time, would not be too much to handle alone in case of necessity."

Alden's skills as a designer were matched by his ability to promote his designs. His *Malabars* were built for his own use, sailed as a floating advertisement, and then sold after a year or two. He was strictly a designer, contracting his boats out to a variety of yards along the East Coast, but mostly in Maine.

He was especially good at designing and selling boats made to an existing design, farming out the work to yards in Maine, where, with the decline in commercial fishing, there were boatbuilders eager for work. In advertisements run in the yachting press, stock designs were offered "ready for delivery." So successful were Alden's designs that some yards built boats on spec, for immediate delivery. Alden defined the production design house, separate from the wood shavings of the boat yard.

In big boats, especially schooners, it was Alden who set the pace, and the growing fraternity of offshore sailors bought his boats in large quantities. The Alden schooner, for production purposes, became "standardized" at 43 feet as either a keel or a centerboard boat, and literally dozens of them were launched along the Maine coast.

Smaller boats weren't ignored; using his skill as a salesman, Alden capitalized on the Malabar name and put out a line of boats known as the Malabar Junior. The first of these, launched in 1925, was the *Little Warrior*, Design Number 243. A gaff sloop, it had round bows that summoned memories of the Friendship sloop, and measured 29 feet, 6 inches overall, with a waterline of 23 feet, 2 inches. When *Little Warrior* was first launched, the design was known only as Number 243. When, a year later, the design became available with a bermudan rig (as Design Number 271), it became known as a Malabar Junior.

The beam of the Malabar Junior series fell very nicely into the 3:1 ratio of the Friendship sloop formula,

and it sold for the very reasonable price of $1,800 in 1925 dollars, which is about $17,650 in today's money, truly a "people's boat."

The first boats built on the lines of *Little Warrior* came with a minimum of brightwork to be maintained, a 5-gallon tank for water, and an engine that could be started with a hand crank. Auxiliary engines, in those days, were truly auxiliary; the *Little Warrior* came with 570 square feet of sail, although subsequent models were rigged with slightly less sail, on the order of 550 square feet, with a displacement of 12,190 pounds and a cast-iron external keel of 3,405 pounds, for a ballast ratio of just over 35 percent. Designed to carry a gaff rig, a bermudan rig was an option; a year later the boat was subtly refined and the bermudan rig became standard. It was this bermudan boat, Design Number 271, that was the first of the production Malabar Juniors.

The production Malabar Juniors were slightly larger than Little Warriors. Design Number 271 measured 30 feet overall, with the waterline extended by an inch and the beam by just half an inch. The draft, up to 5 feet, 1/2 inch, was partly due to the greater ballast, up 1,395 pounds to 4,800 pounds. The increased displacement brought the ballast ratio down to just over 26 percent.

The Malabar Juniors were a success.; 59 were built, all of them recognizable but varying slightly in size, displacement, and sail area. Alberg penned the last of them, Design Number 762, in December 1944, at which point the Juniors had grown to 32 feet, 6 inches overall, displacing 11,650 pounds with a ballast ratio of just over 24 percent.

As was usual with Alden, he had one of the Malabar Juniors built for his personal use. One of three boats of Design Number 599, it was built as a yawl. Like the later 762 design, Alberg drew Alden's boat as well.

The Alden yard was more of an atelier at times, with Alden making suggestions, sketching changes in existing designs, and turning the final stages over to one of his staff. The quality of the people who worked with

Alden is the stuff of legend: Alberg, Howard Chapelle, Sam Crocker, Charles Schock, and Clifford Swain were among the more well known. Olin Stephens was nearly hired, early in his career, but Alden, upon seeing Stephens' portfolio, which included a design for a meter boat, turned him down. Alden had little interest at the time in designing boats built to the International Rule, and by the time they met again, after sailing to Bermuda together in the 1928 race on *Malabar IX* and racing on Alden's Q-class *Hope*, Stephens was busy elsewhere.

There is an element of irony here, as Alden designed *Hope* to the Universal Rule for his personal use.

The boats of the East Coast could easily fill a book, and any less exhaustive treatment of the subject involves selectivity. Most of the foregoing boats had their origins in work boats, and that is a large part of the reason for their selection. Large or small, function decided form in the working boats, and when sailors began to go to sea for pleasure, it was to work boats they looked for design and seaworthiness. ✳

A League of Their Own

Sailboats of the Lake Region

Between the vast stretches of the Pacific Ocean, with its rugged, nearly harbor-free coast and the Atlantic Ocean, with its numerous harbors, bays, and inlets, lies an area with vastly more shoreline than both coasts put together. Largely ignored by coastal sailors, either through regional pride or willful ignorance, the inland lakes and the Great Lakes offer sailing of surpassing beauty and challenge. Long races over water with a temperament, such as the Chicago–Macinac Race, the Trans-Superior, and the Port Huron–Macinac, have given even the best ocean racers ample challenge. The Chicago–Macinac, begun in 1898, has tested sailors for over a hundred years.

When sailors think of sailing in the inland lakes, they usually think of scows—numerous, challenging, and unique to that part of the United States. While along the East Coast, and to a lesser extent the West Coast, there were working boats that could serve as design antecedents, in the Great Lakes area the boats tended to resemble those on the coast. As one might expect, most of the first boats used in the lakes were made at yards on the East Coast, although this changed as boatbuilding became an industry in the heartland.

In Detroit, yachting had an early start. The Detroit Yacht Club, founded in 1839 as a rowing club, is the oldest extant yacht club in the United States. It held its first regatta in 1842.

A scows are still the "big boats" of the scow fleet, at 38 feet overall, and are usually raced with a crew of seven. The starting line action can be intense, without a bowman calling clearance. *Patrick Dunsworth*

Two boat styles developed there. One of them, a centerboard cat ketch, descended from small Scandinavian fishing boats, and was similar to the Mackinaw boat, a type that evolved from working boats used all around the upper Great Lakes. As testimony to this craft's seaworthiness, Sir Earnest Shackleton used a 23-foot boat of this type in his epic journey from the Antarctic to South Georgia Island, a journey of nearly 800 miles.

THE V-BOTTOM CATBOAT

The other boat developed in the Detroit area was a V-bottom catboat, 22 feet long, which was part of the yacht club's racing fleet. The class was very popular, and the racing in it so active that, in 1909, President Taft presented a cup in the club's annual competition. These

boats were raced with a gaff rig initially, but converted to a bermudan rig in the 1920s.

Charles E. Mower designed many of these early catboats, later known as Taft Cup boats; Toledo, Ohio, designers and builders R. A. and A. W. Luedtke designed refined versions. The Luedtkes were instrumental in the change to a bermudan rig, raising the height of the mast, adding a small cuddy, and installing inside ballast to accommodate the added sail area. Taft Cup boats generally were owned by the club, and competitors changed boats regularly. They were raced with a two-person crew.

Boats built to the Universal Rule, especially the R-class, were popular. R-class boats, approximately equivalent to the International Class 6-meters, were roughly 38 feet overall, with a waterline of approximately 25 feet. The numbers are inexact because the various measurements were all put into a formula: give a little here, take a little there; the numbers had to add up to, in the case of the R-class boats, 20 feet. Fleets of R boats were raced at the Detroit and Toledo yacht clubs and other yacht clubs on the eastern Great Lakes, as well as the rest of the Great Lakes.

THE SCOW

But it is the scow that is really the boat of the inland lakes. Scows showed up so near the turn of the century that, to discuss them with any thoroughness, we will have to look at the last few years of the nineteenth century to more fully understand the first years of the twentieth.

The scow form has been around a long time. Scows were used as cargo boats, hunting boats, and as canal barges. With their rectangular shape, flat bottoms, and squared-off bow and stern, they served the purpose of carrying the maximum load in the minimum, easiest-to-build size. The development of the scow is well documented in *The History of the Inland Lake Yachting Association*, by Thomas A. Hodgson, from which much of the information that follows has been taken. (Readers interested

"TAFT CUP CATBOATS"

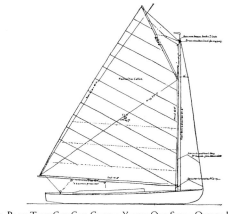

SAIL PLAN TAFT CUP CAT CLASS—YACHT *OLD SAM*—ONE OF DETROIT'S
FASTEST BOATS
Designed by Charles D. Mower

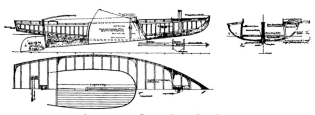

ARRANGEMENT PLAN—TAFT CUP CATS
Designed by Charles D. Mower

The Taft Cup catboat was one of the fastest boats sailed at the Detroit YC, and it was noted for its seaworthiness as well as speed. The large centerboard and huge barn-door rudder did much to alleviate the usual problems of a catboat's lee helm when hard pressed. This particular boat, *Old Sam*, was reputed to be one of the fastest of the Taft Cup class. From *Sailing Craft*, by Edwin J. Schoettle

in full exposition of this boat could do no better than consult this book.)

It is generally agreed that Nathanael Herreschoff took the first step to making the early scow shape into a racing boat, with his scow named *Alfrida*. St. Paul businessman and sailor Lucius Pond Ordway purchased the boat in 1896 for a sailing friend named Milton Griggs. *Alfrida* was built in the manner of a canoe, with continuous ribs athwartships and no keelson. It was gaff-rigged, with a bowsprit over 20 percent the length of the boat itself, and long overhangs.

Another designer influential in developing the scow was George Herrick Duggan, a Canadian bridge engineer by trade. Duggan designed boats with hull shapes very much in the scow form. A gradual trend toward the racing scow shape had been evolving, under the influence of the Seawanhaka Rule, in which a boat's waterline length and sail area determined its rating. Thus, a boat with long overhangs (and a relatively short length on the waterline when at rest) and a huge sail area would be rated as a "short" boat. When heeled, the waterline became much longer, of course, and the scow shape dictated a considerable angle of heel when under sail, thus making the boat effectively longer.

Other designers, such as William Gardner and Arthur Keith, designed and built scows on the coast, where they competed under the Seawanhaka Rule. Gardner's scow-shaped (but ballasted) *Cartoon*, built in 1898, was 25 feet long, with a 10-foot beam and a displacement of 7,168 pounds. Keith built the very scowlike *Hostess* in 1899, measuring 40 feet overall with a beam 6 feet at the bow and 8 feet at the stern, and a sail area of 1,023 square feet. Scow development on the coast and in the inland

waters prior to the turn of the twentieth century proceeded along somewhat parallel lines, but the boat's shape worked best in protected waters, making it ideal for racing and, by extension, development in the inland racing scene.

In 1899, shortly after Griggs began to race *Alfrida*, Ordway, not to be outdone, commissioned a boat from a local builder to be built along the lines of the boats designed by Charles Reed, of the St. Paul firm of Reed and Stem, which would later design New York City's Grand Central Station. Ordway christened the boat *Yankee*, and it seems that with this boat, the scow was truly

The A scows were the biggest of the scow classes, and this one, with its balloon reacher, shows typical scow form, heeling for minimal wetted area.

John O. Irvine collection

born, a final development of the form envisioned by Herreshoff with his *Alfrida*. Duggan himself is reported to have said that *Yankee* was an "all-out scow."

Certainly the measurements bear this out. *Yankee* was 35 feet overall, with a beam of 7 feet, 8 inches and a draft, if that's not too much of a word for it, of only 6 inches. Only the centerboard kept *Yankee* from sliding hopelessly to leeward. While other inland racing boats of that era looked similar, they had far less beam, and relied on ballast rather than crew weight to keep them upright.

Inland boatbuilders had been inching toward the form on their own. John O. Johnson of White Bear Lake, Minnesota, was a well-known boatbuilder, and possessed considerable skills and ingenuity in other fields. He invented a rotary snowplow and built an airplane on which he made the first powered flight in Minnesota, taking off from a frozen lake in January 1910. To Johnson goes the credit for the next crucial step in the evolution of the scow: bilge boards. In 1896, Johnson built a scowlike boat called *Weirdling*, aptly

By 1900, racing was fast and furious under the ILYA banner. Scows had shown themselves to be so successful that several of the faster boats began to look somewhat alike. Many of them were roughly the same size as *Yankee*, but the real quest was for light weight. The 20-footer *Problem*, for example, weighed in at only 600 pounds. One of the first things the ILYA did after the first set of rules was to formulate scantlings to ensure that boats had a certain minimum strength.

The year 1900 brought significant events elsewhere. On the Great Salt Lake, Captain David Lazarus Davis, the first commodore of the Great Salt Lake Yacht Club, built his second catamaran, named *Cambria*—the same name as his first, built in 1877. The original *Cambria* was reputed to be the first catamaran launched in the United States. *Cambria II* was 65 feet overall, with hulls 41 feet long, and was 24 feet on the beam. It carried 1,500 square feet of sail on the main and mizzen.

The expanse of the Great Salt Lake, which varied in size considerably according to the vagaries of rainfall, was the home of an active sailing fleet that had its ups and downs roughly coinciding with the lake's rise and fall. At the turn of the century, the lake began to rise, and after a lag period of a few years, by 1925, the fleets were out. A large building, passing for a marina, (among its other uses), called Saltair was built, and in 1932 the club built a clubhouse beneath Saltair's south pier, assembled for the tidy sum of $200 (still a bargain in 2000, at $2,526).

In 1902, the Inter-Lake Yacht Racing Association (I-LYA), an umbrella organization primarily concerned with the Great Lakes, adopted the Yacht Racing Union rule, superseding the Seawanhaka Rule.

Two years later the I-LYA went on to ban professional sailors at the helm of racing boats, but did allow what they termed "reformed" professionals, whatever that might be. The I-LYA was formed in 1885 in Cleveland, Ohio. The same year, it began the annual Put-In-Bay regatta, a gala event that had its heyday in the regatta of 1912. It lasted for a full month, celebrating the centennial

On many occasions, sailors sent their boats by rail, with the final delivery done on horse-drawn trailers, as with this E scow. The wood would often dry out and the seams would open.

Thomas Hodgson collection

named for the boat's scow-like, previously unseen, shape. Realizing that scows, when sailing as designed, were at a considerable angle of heel, he put in twin boards, bilge boards, in the parlance of scows, extending out at an angle from the hull that would have them nearly vertical when the boat was heeled.

THE INLAND LAKE
YACHTING ASSOCIATION

With just three years left in the nineteenth century, the Inland Lake Yachting Association (ILYA) was formed, the result of a meeting of between 17 and 19 sailing clubs (there is some confusion in the historical record) from four states. They agreed on a common measuring rule for members' boats and organized their first regatta.

of Commodore Perry's victory over the British in the Battle of Lake Erie during the war of 1812. The prize purse amounted to a total of $25,000 in 1912 dollars, a sum equivalent to just over $44,000 today.

In 1907, the I-LYA adopted the Universal Rule, the fourth time in 24 years it had changed the rating system for the association, but this time the change put it in harmony with many of the other regional associations and clubs.

The Yacht Racing Union (YRU) of the Great Lakes, founded in 1896, is another umbrella organization for sailors of the Great Lakes. The member associations of the YRU are the Lake Yacht Racing Association, the Lake Superior Yachting Association, the Lake Huron Yachting Association, the Lake Michigan Sail Racing Association, the Detroit Regional Yachting Association, and the I-LYA. The first major cup associated with the YRU was to become known as the Yacht Racing Union Cup, and the first race, between P-class boats, was held in 1912. World War I interrupted the smooth flow of what had been planned to be a biennial event for "substantial yachts," and the cup wasn't awarded again until 1922. The Deed of Gift for the cup, presented by Commodore S. O. Richardson of the Toledo Yacht Club, was amended at that time to allow R-boats, a more popular class on the lakes.

The people who began the YRU were pivotal to the development of sailboat racing in the United States. Among them were George W. Gardner and Ernest

(*top opposite*) The 32-foot Class B boats eventually disappeared, as they were too near the 28-foot E scow in size. These two gaff-rigged Bs, with their impossibly long spinnaker poles, are racing at one of the last of the international B-class events, when the White Bear Lake YC raced against the Royal St. Louis YC of Montreal, Canada. *John O. Irvine collection*

Two A scows, in the years between the adoption of the bumpkin and the adoption of the bermudan rig, match each other on a run, flying both spinnaker and headsail, which must have complicated tacking. *John O. Irvine collection*

Radder, of Cleveland, Ohio. Gardner was a founder of the Cleveland Yacht Club in 1878 and the I-LYA in 1885. Radder, also of the Cleveland YC, helped found the United States Sailing Association, now U.S. Sailing, at a meeting in the Fifth Avenue Hotel in New York City in 1897.

Back in the waters of the ILYA, the 1900 regatta, held on Lake Geneva, Wisconsin, was a resounding success, lasting a full week with a tent city erected on the shores to house the racers. But it was at the ILYA's special meeting that an event of far greater significance took place. The members voted to require, in the 1901 regatta, that "both captain and crew of all competing boats shall be amateurs." This Corinthian ideal nipped in the bud the practice of "checkbook" sailboat racing in the ILYA, ensuring that, regardless of the money spent to have a winning boat, everyone in it would be sailing for the love of the sport and not for the money.

—— EXPANSION OF THE SCOW CLASS ——

The year 1900 was also the year when scantlings began to be regulated, and new classes were formed, based on length and sail area. Lacking imagination, two classes were designated: "A" and "B." The A scow was to be no longer than 38 feet, and the B no longer than 32 feet. In 1905 a third class, called, of course, "C," was formulated, specifying length, beam, and crew weight but not, significantly, sail area. The C boat was limited to no more than 25 feet in length, beam could be no less than 7 feet, and the freeboard was limited to 14 inches. Crew weight was limited to 500 pounds, and the cat-rigged boat was limited to one centerboard and one rudder.

Next was the "D" boat, this one created by what amounted to a dissident group of eight yacht clubs from southeastern Wisconsin and Illinois that did not like having to travel to Oshkosh every year for the ILYA regattas. They formed the Northwestern Regatta Association (NRA), adopted the ILYA's A and B scows, and then formulated the first class to have bilge boards, this

one even shorter than the C scow, at 25 feet long. The D scow, 18 feet long, would carry 225 square feet of sail in a cat rig. The D scow became very popular almost immediately, with 24 of them showing up for the NRA's first regatta in 1906.

The NRA's naming of its new scow class created some confusion among sailors, since a knockabout boat already existed on Lake Geneva called the C-class. The association persisted in the name for the scow, though, as they wanted to maintain a continuity of nomenclature.

When they made a rule modification in 1908, strengthening the scantlings and allowing either bilge boards or a centerboard, but not twin rudders, they had a chance to change the name, but the NRA members felt that would only create further confusion.

The ILYA discovered that some of its members were racing in NRA events, and some regattas had too few participants. The NRA as well was finding that the pie

(*opposite*) When the E scows all get together to race, even Wisconsin's Lake Mendota can become crowded. With a crew of three, a hull weighing just 965 pounds, and 873 square feet of downwind sail area, it's one of the fastest rides on the inland lakes.

Patrick Dunsworth

In 1924, Johnson Boat Works built one of the two E-scow prototypes, this one exhibiting a canoe bow that was later changed to a more scow-like squared-off bow. Later modifications included making the sail area larger, from 285 square feet to 300 in 1932.

Thomas Hodgson collection

A bit of calm air affords a chance to examine the rigging of this older E scow. Note the clubfooted jib and the complex set of stays needed to support the fractional rig on the wood mast. This boat has twin rudders. The class rules allowed either single or twin rudders, but the advantages of two rudders when the boat was at its typical angle of heel made the single rudder uncompetitive. *Thomas Hodgson collection*

(pages 74-75) The X-boat, introduced as the Cub in 1936, is one of the most active classes for junior racing in the inland lakes. Now made of fiberglass, only minor changes have been made in the original design. *Patrick Dunsworth*

was possibly divided too small for the number of sailors. Merger was in the air, and in 1916 the two joined forces, capped by the ILYA incorporating and selling shares of stock. It was a small initial offering, with just 15 shares, at $5 each.

With the outbreak of World War I, racing stopped, and there was no regatta in 1917 or 1918. By 1919, two months after the Treaty of Versailles, the annual ILYA regatta was again held, and in 1920 racing was bigger than ever.

The year 1920 marked the acceptance of the bermudan rig, but not before much debate; the new triangular sails would be permitted for championship races, but changing rigs during the regatta was forbidden.

—— ADVENT OF THE BOAT TRAILER ——

An important invention for the racing scene was what amounted to the boat trailer. Boats were transported to races by a variety of means. Fitting a long

scow hull into a boxcar, through its door in the middle, was difficult at best. A horse and wagon was slow, and the cars of the 1920s were not designed to drag a boat that equaled or surpassed their own weight, but trailer they did. Early photographs of trailered boats show an amazing collection of home-built rigs, with wheels salvaged from cars, bicycles, farm wagons, and anything else suitably round.

The inland racers were not bound by the traditions of the clubs back east, and no better evidence of that can be found than with a quick look at the number of women who competed in the regattas. They competed boat-for-boat, sailing against the men sailors. In 1921, Ruth Bovey, sailing her boat named *Marchioness*, won the ILYA's annual regatta. In the 1930s, there were 100 women, as both skipper and crew, in the annual regattas.

Women were not unheard of in other inland lake sailing venues. In the 1905 Port Huron–Macinac Race, sponsored jointly by the Detroit Country Club and the Chicago Yacht Club, the yacht *Eileen*, skippered by Evelyn Wright, entered the race with an all-women crew. Just to show she was serious, Wright did it again in 1908.

By the 1920s, ILYA sailors had been voting with their feet, or perhaps their tiller hand, in their choice of boats to race. The B scow, similar to the A in many ways, had been declining in popularity for 10 years, and the A, all 38 feet of it, was an expensive boat to build, race, and maintain. The C, small enough to be popular, wasn't as exciting to race, being cat-rigged and necessarily limited in sail area. A curious clause in the rules also forbade anyone who skippered an A scow from competing in a C scow. It was time for a new boat, which logic would say would be the D scow, but the NRA had an 18-foot cat-rigged sloop it called the D-class. No doubt remembering the confusion resulting from having two

C-class boats, the club chose the next letter, dubbing the new boat the E scow.

THE E SCOW

The basic design parameters called for a boat that was smaller than the A, with a three-person crew. In November 1923, the design committee of the ILYA decided on minimum and maximum lengths for the E scow: 27 feet, 9 inches to 28 feet overall; beam 6 feet, 6 inches to 6 feet, 9 inches; depth between 16 and 17 inches; and sail area no greater than 285 square feet. The centerboard was to be a piece of boiler-plate steel 5/16-inch thick, and either single or twin rudders were accepted.

Two prototypes were built, one each by the Palmer Boat Company in Fontana, Wisconsin, and the Johnson Boat Works of White Bear Lake, Minnesota. The resulting boats were to be raffled off to encourage the new fleet. The new boats cost $750 dollars, equal to $7,570 in 2000. At least five other E scows were built during this inaugural year, bringing the fleet up to seven boats.

The E scows sailed for only a short time before the ILYA considered a refinement of the design. During a meeting in November 1924, ILYA board members voted to allow bilge boards, but there was some concern that the owners of centerboard boats would feel a bit hard done by having to modify a new boat to stay competitive. The board then considered a motion to allow the ILYA to reimburse the owners for half of the expense, and defray the cost of shipping the boat to the builder by giving the owners an additional $100 (that's just a few dollars over $1,000 today). When a survey of the clubs revealed that at least eight new boats would be ordered with this provision, the motion passed handily. Both the ILYA and those contemplating ordering the new boats felt it was important the association show a sincere interest in keeping the older boats competitive as an aid in nurturing the new class.

By 1928, there were 32 E boats on the starting line at the annual regatta, and the price of a new boat had remained remarkably constant. You could sail away a new E scow for between $850 and $875, or $8,538 to $8,790 in 2000 dollars.

The design of the E was not cast in bronze, but nearly so. Efforts to introduce exotic or expensive gadgetry were kept to an absolute minimum. The result was a fleet that grew steadily, and old boats retained their value.

THE GREAT DEPRESSION

With the onset of the Great Depression, sailing continued, but at a diminished rate. The smaller classes saw their numbers diminished, but the bigger boats, the A scows, were nearly as numerous as ever. A survey of the owners of these boats shows sailors with such family

The Luders 16, a hot performer, had its performance increased by the use of molded plywood in its construction. Even with a ballast ratio of 50 percent, the weight of two crew members on the windward rail is necessary. *Rosenfeld collection, Mystic, Connecticut*

Lake won the C-scow class. Kay took the helm, her sister Caroline handled the bilge boards, and Maynard "Mike" Meyer from Pewaukee, Wisconsin, trimmed the mainsheet, on a boat named *Black Rhythm*.

In other areas of the country, the decade of the 1930s had mixed effects. The Great Salt Lake had begun to shrink again. Sailboats were particularly hard hit. Because of their greater draft, they had to be moored quite some distance from shore, as the gently sloping bottom gained depth very gradually. The mooring was unprotected, sailors had to make a long trip by rowboat to get to their boats, and when storms came up, the moored boats were hit by the full force of the lake's waves. These factors contributed to a drastic reduction in the number of sailboats until the middle of the 1960s, when the lake finally began to rise again.

JUNIOR RACING IN THE DEPRESSION

In the 1930s, there were only a few clubs with active junior sailing programs. A few of these clubs had special boats for the junior sailors, but for the most part, children learned to sail by crewing on smaller boats or by fiddling about in a rowboat set up with a sail of some kind. The ILYA, however, had no boats that were designed for junior sailors as a class. In 1932, Len Lilly Sr., of the same Lilly family that produced the championship Lilly sisters, commissioned John O. Johnson of the Johnson Boat Works to design and build a boat especially for junior sailors. It would be small, stable, easy to sail, and, of course, inexpensive. Johnson produced a hard-chine centerboard dinghy measuring 15 feet, 6 inches long, with a reverse sheer and a flat, reversed transom. Four of the prototypes were built and sailed through the 1933 season.

names as Pillsbury, Kimberly, Hannaford, Weyerhaeuser, and Ordway. Wealth of that scale, while still affected by the depression, never entirely deserted its owners.

Even with the reduced numbers, racing continued. In the 1932 annual regattas, for example, 38 C scows were at the starting line, and the women were continuing to compete. In the 1934 regatta, the Lilly sisters of White Bear

By 1934, the ILYA was convinced that a special boat for the junior class was needed, and by the end of 1934 it adopted a design by T. R. Hedengren. This boat, to be called the Cub, was slightly larger than the Johnson prototype, at 16 feet, with a more conventional sheer line. The hard-chine sloop-rigged centerboarder carried 120.2 square feet of sail, with a diminutive clubfooted jib

of only 25 square feet. Stability was inherent in the design, with a beam-to-length ratio of just 2.58 on a beam measurement of 6 feet, 3 inches.

The new boat was well received, becoming an official ILYA class by October 1935. Part of the success can be attributed to the design's simplicity. It was also inexpensive to build: the Johnson Boat Works sold Cubs for $250, or $3,139 in today's money, with just $14 ($175) tacked on for shipping. A home-built version could be put together for around $100 ($1,255 today), which was even better, as the depression was in full swing.

Some of the people building Cubs made minor changes, so in 1936 a standard set of lines was approved, with a few minor refinements added. The mast was lengthened, the boom shortened, and the point of maximum beam was moved slightly aft—changes that made the final version more nearly like the early Johnson prototype than the Hedengren design.

With this rather extensive field-testing of the design, the final version of the Cub was a genuinely good boat. Class rules specified the boat to be wet-sailed, so Cubs were always at the dock, ready for junior sailors to take out whenever they wished. And sail they did. A young sailor from Delavan, Wisconsin, named Buddy Melges made enough money giving 10-cent sailboat rides to his friends that he was able to buy a new sail for his boat—which probably needed it after all those dime rides.

The events of Sunday morning, December 7, 1941, at Pearl Harbor,

(*opposite*) This Thistle, planing nicely in a good breeze, is an early molded-plywood model. The Thistle's hull shape affords a lot of room for crew, and it is as much at home daysailing the family as it is on the race course. The Thistle is the second-most-popular one-design, after the Laser. *Rosenfeld collection, Mystic, Connecticut*

The M-16, small, fast, and the first star of the Melges-designed fleet, has some of the sophistication of the larger scows. Note the bilge boards and sheet stopper. *Patrick Dunsworth*

Hawaii, and the entrance of the United States into World War II put a quick but temporary halt to the sailing activities of all the clubs and fleets across the country. Yet one ILYA class did remain competitive throughout the war, evidence, perhaps, of its affordability. The Cubs continued to race, although gas rationing eventually made it impossible to transport the boats to the races. The solution was to have the hosting club provide boats for the visiting sailors, reducing the need for gas to a school bus full of young sailors.

LUDERS L16

Toward the end of the war years, Luders Marine Construction Company, which had been building hot-molded plywood life rafts to be air-dropped to downed pilots, began to look for boats for the civilian market that could be built by this method. Luders chose the Luders 16, first built in 1934, but the factory thought a molded plywood version of the L16 would rejuvenate a nearly moribund stick-built wood design by using their new construction method.

The new version was 26 feet, 4 inches overall, and

16 feet, 4 inches on the waterline. The beam was 5 feet, 9 inches and displacement 3,200 pounds. The L16 had a big genoa, one of the first of the deck sweepers that were to become so popular, at 180 percent. Total working sail area was 207 square feet.

The first seven of the new L16s were ordered in 1945 by a group of Chicago sailors, at the recommendation of Clare Udell. The price in 1945 was $1,950 ($18,680 today), which made it a relatively expensive boat for its size. Despite this, the boat's popularity grew, expanding from that first Chicago fleet to both coasts—especially Long Island Sound—as well as the Gulf Coast.

THE CUB AND CLASS X

The ILYA continued to have problems with the names of some of its classes. The Cub is a good example. Clubs in the northern region of the ILYA began to call it the Class X. In the southern part, there was already a Class X boat, this one a scowlike sloop. Despite a 1940 resolution from the ILYA declaring the Cub to be a Cub, and not Class X, the little junior sailer was still referred to as Class X. By 1947, in order to establish alphabetic uniformity for ILYA classes, the group's taxonomists "went north," reversing the 1940 edict and renaming the Cub class as Class X.

With the war over, people wanted to go sailing more than ever. For a short time, the hot-molded-plywood construction method looked like the way of the future. In just a few years, however, it was displaced by fiberglass, which was lighter, cheaper, more easily shaped, and required less tooling.

In 1945, at the annual Put-In-Bay regatta, a boat appeared that was to be one of the great success stories of one-design racing. Gordon K. Douglass drew the boat during the war years, and he rebuilt the first one of double-planked construction. His idea had been to produce the boat as a hot-molded-plywood boat, so the lines were drawn with that construction in mind.

The 16-foot MC scow was conceived by Harry Melges Sr. in 1950, based on the M-16 hull, but slightly lighter with more sail area. Harry and son Buddy designed the fiberglass MC familiar to today's sailors in 1965. Patrick Dunsworth

The M-20 scow, another speedster from the Melges Works, was so fast that it took seven years for it to be accepted by the ILYA as a class. Its tunnel-shaped hull, which considerably reduced wetted area when even slightly heeled, was the stumbling block. With bilge boards and twin rudders, it is a sophisticated racing boat, carrying 376 square feet of downwind sail and only 595 pounds displacement.

Patrick Dunsworth

THE THISTLE

The new boat, which Douglass called a Thistle, was just 17 feet overall and on the waterline, was an open dinghy, 6 feet in beam, displacing 515 pounds with a sail area of 191 square feet in the job and main, with a 220-square-foot spinnaker. The weighted centerboard dinghy had a rounded hull that carried the boat over the waves rather than through them, and the rockered underwater profile made it a planing hull. Douglass, with his wife as crew, entered the boat in the Universal Class for that 1945 regatta. This was a catch-all class, set up to allow boats too low in numbers to make a fleet or have their own class, and entrants were handicapped to the Universal Rule. The winds were strong, estimated at 40 miles an hour with gusts pushing even higher.

Spectators gave the boat slim chances. It looked like an enlarged version of an International 14, and Lake Erie's notorious square waves, a product of the lake's shallow water, were expected to prevent it from being a threat.

Douglass and his wife dominated the fleet, which consisted entirely of larger boats, including a big schooner, numerous keelboats, and a 22-square-meter.

testament to the soundness of the design and the class association's strict adherence to the original lines of the boat design, hull number 1 still competes, and has won national championships against boats more than 30 years its junior.

The years right after World War II saw the development of more new classes in the ILYA, and the beginning of what might be called a sailing dynasty-cum-boat-yard. Harry Melges Sr. had worked for several boat companies before World War II, and in 1945 he set up his own business. He wanted only to make boats, and not to be involved with the shoreside service business, so he chose Zenda, Wisconsin, which was several miles from Lake Geneva, for his new boat yard. He went into business with partner Ephraim Banning. They called the new boatbuilding business Mel-Ban Boat Works. The yard's first boats were flat-bottomed rowboats. Over the winter of 1946–1947, Mel-Ban built four C scows, and following some success on the race course, began to build Cs on a regular basis. Some two years later, Melges bought out Banning and changed the name to Melges Boat Works.

Harry Sr. and Harry Jr.—known as Buddy—soon began to build E scows and then A scows. The Melges Boat Works began to make its own designs. The first of these was a 16-foot, reverse-sheer sloop it called the M-16. It was, in effect, a scaled-down D or E scow, with bilge boards, twin rudders, and a wide variety of sail controls. To promote the new design, Buddy took an M-16 to the ILYA's annual regatta in 1950, tied it to the dock, and let anyone who was curious take it out for a ride.

By 1953, there were 21 of the new boats on the water, reasonably good considering the ILYA had not given the M-16 its imprimatur, categorizing it as an experimental fleet until 1959. When the boat won official acceptance as a sanctioned class, other yards began to build it.

Melges then put out another boat, the M-20. The ILYA was reluctant to sanction this boat because of a slight tunnel shape to its hull profile. A rule adopted in

His new boat got up on a plane and roared around the 15-mile offshore triangular course, finishing 20 minutes ahead of the second-place boat.

Douglass was fully occupied after the regatta, taking people for rides in his new boat. He put the boat into production soon afterward, using hot-molded plywood for both fully constructed boats and the ones he sold as a kit. Later, the boat went into fiberglass production. As

1899 specifically prohibited this design feature in response to a boat named *Dominion*, designed by Duggan. The *Dominion* had what was nearly a catamaran shape to its hull, with two rounded bilges that allowed the boat when heeled to have a long, slim hull shape. The boat was so fast the ratings committees did what rating committees usually do when faced with a winning innovation: they outlawed it. Not until 1966, by which time Melges was building more than one M-20 a week, was the boat accepted as an ILYA-sanctioned class.

— FIBERGLASS CONSTRUCTION COMES OF AGE —

Fiberglass, taking over the boat industry by the 1950s, was slightly slower in finding acceptance with the inland boat builders. The Stamm Boat Company was the first of the inland boaters to adopt fiberglass, making X boats and the first fiberglass C scow. Some yards continued to make wooden scows until the mid-1970s and later.

By the 1960s, in conjunction with a boom in recreational sailing on the inland lakes and the unprecedented ease of building boats out of fiberglass, there seemed to be boat factories at every lake. "Factories" is something of an aggrandizement, as many of these businesses were little more than a garage or a barn, but they did turn out boats, and for a very affordable price. In 1968, for example, Fibre Fab Corporation would sell you a C scow, with the hull guaranteed for one year, for $2,150, equal to $16,190 today. Scows had truly arrived. In 1973, the three main builders of C scows together sold 115 boats.

The history of American sailboats in the waters between the coasts is one of continuous innovation, matched to the waters they sail in. While big boats were sailed on the Great Lakes, these boats usually had their origins in saltwater. It was on the smaller lakes that the scows developed to their fullest potential, producing sailors of world-championship ability. Managing a boat with the performance potential of a scow, sailing it in the constantly shifting winds that are a characteristic of inland lakes, and reading the shifts and puffs caused by land features, afternoon thunderstorms, and the uneven heating of fields adjoining the lake, can produce sailors who are easily the equal of any sailor raised on saltwater. ✳

(*opposite*) On board an E scow as it chases the competition makes for a perfect day on the many inland lakes where scows reign. *Patrick Dunsworth*

At the ILYA's 1946 annual regatta, the A scows fly older, triangular spinnakers. The letters indicate the club the owner is a member of; the letters chosen read the same on both sides of the sail, a system that worked well until the ILYA ran out of reversible letters. *Thomas Hodgson collection*

Racing Plays a Pivotal Role

West Coast Sailboats

Most of the West Coast's first European settlers got there by sailing. As they had on the East Coast, recreational sailors turned to enjoyment boats and skills they had developed for work. Making a living came first; sailing for fun and competition followed. The transition from work to play, usually on the same boats, was at times a tenuous one, with the boundary indistinct.

In Seattle, the southern terminus of the lucrative Alaskan trade, full-rigged sailing vessels showed up regularly. While blessed with protected waters and many small islands, Puget Sound's winds tend to die off in the summer, yet the Sound was part of a thriving yachting scene dating to the earliest days of the twentieth century.

In San Francisco Bay, large scows, schooner-rigged and some of them over 100 feet long, carried everything from loads of hay to bricks, and when these ungainly craft weren't carrying cargo, racing them became a regular event. Scows raced anything with sails, and the betting was at least as exciting as the racing itself. The San Francisco Yacht Club was founded in 1869, and until the 1950s, San Francisco was probably the leading area for recreational sailing on the West Coast, blessed with good winds and a sheltered bay.

The PC class was fast, with a fine entry to the bow and a deep, comfortable, and secure cockpit. Designed in 1929, the boat is still actively sailed on the West Coast. The Y-shaped device aft of the traveler is the boom crutch; PCs do not have a topping lift. *Bob Grieser*

Photographs of the Chula

Vista One-Design are

nearly as scarce as the

boat itself, which is a

shame, as the boat's

graceful lines and classic

sail plan are lovely to see.

There were 11 of them

built and races were held

monthly. *John Willett*

The West Coast did not lend itself to yachting as easily as the East Coast. Most of the coast is either rocky, with cliffs leading to the ocean's edge, or consists of sandy beaches; missing are sheltered harbors, large bays, or offshore islands in anything like the number on the East Coast. As well, the recreational sailing tended to be more local, with sailors from, say, San Francisco not sailing to San Diego on a regular basis.

In the southern part of California, San Diego's sailing scene at the turn of the twentieth century was, if possible, less organized than that of San Francisco's. A race was usually referred to as a "water carnival," and the boats involved weren't separated by class, design, or purpose. They were all sailboats, and they all raced in an informal, good-natured fashion.

THE CHULA VISTA ONE-DESIGN

The Chula Vista One-Design, a gaff-rigged 27-foot sloop, was designed and built around the turn of the twentieth century by Clem Stose, and at the time was the largest one-design fleet on the entire West Coast. It was built for members of the Chula Vista Yacht Club for the express purpose of racing, a first on the West Coast.

Not only was the Chula Vista One Design the largest of the classes on the West Coast, there is good evidence it is the oldest, according to letters and interviews with people who sailed them and marine historians. Their popularity certainly was a reflection of their sailing qualities, as with any one design fleet. They were very shallow of draft, described by sailers of the time as "two decks and no bottom." Beamy, at 9 feet, 8 inches, they

carried 800 square feet of sail. The first batch of 12 were only $400 each sailaway, equal to $7,200 today.

The boat no longer exists; the only remnant of the Chula Vista One-Design is a mast, discovered in the yard of the granddaughter of one of the early sailors who had been using it as flagpole, and salvaged by John Willet, a local marine historian and a member of the San Diego Tall Ships Society. The boat now survives in a set of lines taken from the few photographs of the boat, painstakingly transferred by dividers and trigonometry to a piece of paper. It awaits rebirth by someone sufficiently enthusiastic about the vanished history of San Diego's sailing to create one and once again grace the waters of San Diego with a living piece of history.

In 1903, the San Diego YC sent a letter to Sir Thomas Lipton, who had gained fame and no small measure of affection among American sailors for his five-times-unsuccessful pursuit of the America's Cup. Lipton was also known for his hobby of donating cups to yacht clubs around the United States, promoting the grand sport of yacht racing. There are Lipton Cups from coast to coast, always lovely silver trophies with plenty of room on the sides to accommodate engraved names of winners.

Lipton was no less generous with the San Diego YC, sending a 32-inch-tall cup that became known as, appropriately enough, the Lipton Cup.

THE LIPTON CUP

For the inaugural race for the Lipton Cup, San Diego YC members organized into a syndicate to have a boat built that would be a suitable, and hopefully winning, competition vessel.

They first contacted Nathanael Herreshoff, but things didn't work out. Perhaps the price was too high, perhaps they felt the "Wizard of Bristol" wouldn't make the right boat for their waters. At any rate, they pooled their resources (if that's not too extreme a term, considering that they came up with a total of $25, roughly $480 today), purchased, and brought to San Diego a

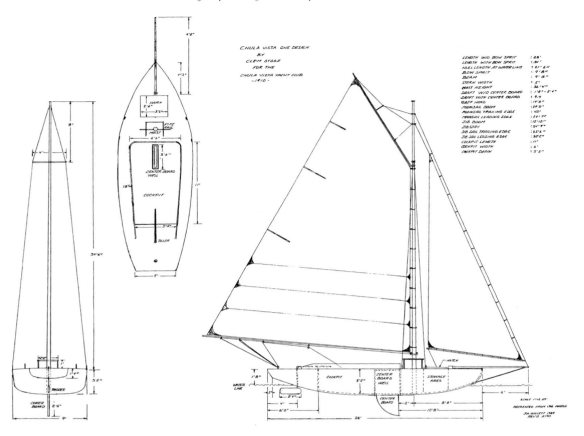

CHULA VISTA ONE DESIGN
BY
CLEM STOSE
FOR THE
CHULA VISTA YACHT CLUB
-1910-

The lines of the 34-foot (including the 6-foot bowsprit) Chula Vista One-Design have been recreated by maritime historian John Willett from photographs and records. *Drawing courtesy John Willett*

Butcher Boy and *Detroit* faced off at the second Lipton Cup race in 1905, with *Detroit* leading as they pass San Diego's Hotel del Coronado. *San Diego Maritime Museum*

START OF "DETROIT" AND "BUTCHER BOY"
OFF CORONADO HOTEL AUGUST 30.
LIPTON CUP RACES 1905. SAN DIEGO, CALIF.
H.R. FITCH. PHOTO.

The 80-foot (including the 21-foot bowsprit) San Francisco scow schooner *Alma* is the grande dame of Bay classics. The boat was named after the daughter of Fred Siemer, who designed and built it in 1891 at his Hunters Point yard in San Francisco Bay. Unusually, its bottom planks are laid athwartships rather than fore-and-aft. With a draft of just 4 feet, *Alma* is not a windward performer, even with the centerboard down. There were once over 400 scow schooners in the Bay; *Alma*, a National Historic Landmark since 1988, is the last. *Mariah's Eyes*

boat that had been very successful racing on the Great Lakes, a 47-foot, 6-inch sloop named *Detroit*.

The *Detroit* did well. Covered with sails and blessed with a sleek hull, the boat won easily, racing against three boats from the South Coast Yacht Club and one from the local Corinthian Yacht Club.

For reasons no longer known, the Chula Vista YC sold *Detroit* to some members of the South Coast YC. This turned out to be a strategic error; following the next race, the Lipton Cup took up residence at the South Coast YC.

A working boat was at the starting line for the 1905 Lipton Cup race—a 30-foot double-ended sloop with the perfectly apt name of *Butcher Boy*. It had been built along the lines of a Columbia River salmon boat, and had spent its working life ferrying meat and other supplies to larger ships lying at anchor in the roads of San Diego harbor. Retired from that rather inglorious but worthwhile calling, *Butcher Boy* was bought and sold many times before it became a racing yacht. No match for the *Detroit*, it was still a crowd favorite, and eventually was restored, after being found languishing in the Los Angeles area.

(*below*) The R-boat *Sir Tom*, designed in 1913 by Ted Geary, is probably the most well known boat in the history of the Seattle YC. Geary was usually *Sir Tom*'s skipper, and its first major victory was the Sir Thomas Lipton Perpetual Challenge Trophy race of 1913. *Ken Ollar*

(*left*) *Butcher Boy*, a prized exhibit at the San Diego Maritime Museum, shows its workboat lineage in the sturdy lines and beefy construction. *San Diego Maritime Museum*

The 37-foot *Mischief*, representing the South Coast YC in the 1906 Lipton Cup race, defeated *Aeolus*. *San Diego YC.*

The gaff sloop *Aeolus* was built as the city of San Diego's entry for the 1906 Lipton Cup race. *San Diego YC.*

The boat was sailed back to San Diego and is now a prized exhibit at the San Diego Maritime Museum.

The Lipton Cup contest continued until 1921, with a number of boats being commissioned especially for the race. *Aeolus*, sponsored by no less than the City of San Diego, was built at San Diego's Jensen's Boat Yard, but was defeated in the 1906 race by *Mischief*, a boat from the South Coast YC. *Aeolus* was later purchased by Alonzo de Jessop and Frank Wyatt of the San Diego YC, who together sailed the boat for years afterward, doing very well in local races.

By 1906, sailing had become relatively well established as a recreational sport, and when Clarence Mac-Farlane of Honolulu arrived in San Francisco on his boat *La Paloma*, his plan was to invite Bay sailors to race to Hawaii. The trick, he felt, was to convince West Coast sailors that the return voyage, beating back from Hawaii, was not so difficult as to rule out the possibility of a downwind race to Hawaii.

His timing could hardly have been worse, at least from the standpoint of San Francisco sailors. The earthquake of 1906 had virtually leveled the city less than a month before, and no one was very interested in discussing a sailboat race.

MacFarlane cast off and sailed down to San Pedro, Los Angeles' harbor town, and was received with more enthusiasm. Not a lot more—two boats signed up for

this first Transpac. One was the 80-foot schooner *Lurline*, then belonging to Captain H. H. Sinclair, commodore of San Diego's South Coast YC. The other was *Anemone*, a 112-foot schooner belonging to Charles Tutt of Colorado Springs, Colorado, and a member of the New York YC. For the record, MacFarlane was last, with *Lurline* taking the honors for that first Transpac, then called the Honolulu Race.

THE SAN DIEGO YACHT CLUB

At the San Diego YC in 1918, a one-design class had been commissioned as well, possibly after seeing the success of the Chula Vista One-Design. There was room for another boat, even another yacht club, as the Chula Vista YC had fallen on hard times, with a series of floods destroying their wharf and eroding the access to the clubhouse. In 1916 a flood filled San Diego's South Bay with

The schooner *Lurline*, belonging at the time to the commodore of the San Diego YC, won the first Transpac in 1906, and again in 1908 and 1912, owned by A. E. Davis. *San Diego* YC

sediment, reducing the water depth even further and making sailing in anything other than the most shallow-drafted boats impossible. This, coupled with the other problems Chula Vista YC had been having, combined to put the club out of business. By 1934 even the clubhouse was gone, dismantled and sold to a saltworks in Baja, Mexico.

Problems with the Chula Vista YC weren't indicative of the state of sailing in San Diego generally, though. Sailing had become pretty well established by the mid-1920s, but it was almost entirely a sport for adults. In 1928 (four years after moving to its new, and present, location on Point Loma), a few members of the San Diego YC felt the club should initiate a junior sailing program.

This was not a universal opinion, but there were enough members who were enthusiastic about it that a junior sailing program was begun. The first order of business was the commissioning of junior-class boats, and a fleet of 10 clinker-built cat-rigged boats (called, variously, Cat Boats and Sea Mews) was built.

THE STARLET

As the fleet aged, club members then had another, smaller boat built, specifically for the junior program. Scaled down and designed after the Star, the boat was called the Starlet, and it was the beginning of one of the most successful junior sailing programs in the country.

Joe Ruski designed the Starlet, 16 feet long with 130 square feet of sail, and included a bulb-type keel, just as on the Star. After building six of them, a design makeover and construction was placed in the hands of George Kettenburg Jr., who, together with his father, ran the Kettenburg Marine boat yard in San Diego.

The Starlet, built to the most attractive price of $125 ($1,250 today) including sails, was an absolute success, and 40 of them were built, providing the junior sailors with a fleet that served them until the 1950s.

Also in the 1920s, Joe Jessop and Ed Peterson of the San Diego YC built the first Star in the San Diego area. This marked the beginning of an illustrious career in Star boat racing for Jessop, who won the Pacific Coast Star Class championship in 1924, 1926, and 1927, and the Star Internationals in 1925, among other events. Stars were then built in fleet quantities by local yards, including the Kettenburg yard.

Mission Bay, originally called False Bay because of its shallow waters, was the neglected northern section of San Diego's bay. The water was deep enough to set up a sailing club, though, and in 1927 the Mission Bay Yacht Club was formed. One of its accomplishments was the founding of the first Lightning fleet in California.

A significant one-design of that era, one that lasted from the late 1920s to the 1950s, was the Pacific Coast One-Design, known as the PC. George Kettenburg Jr. designed the boat in 1929 at the request of Joe Jessop, then commodore of the San Diego YC. The club members wanted a boat that was easier to sail than the Stars and Etchells, and also suitable to take their families out.

Jessop, quoted in a 1994 article in *Sailing* magazine, said, "We decided we wanted larger boats that we could sleep on when we went to Los Angeles and Santa Barbara to attend regattas." Jessop and his committee decided that Kettenburg Jr. was the man for the job. It was to be the first boat Kettenburg had done entirely on his own, and the design worked. It worked so well that, in 1931, the design won the Lipton Cup regatta, which

was open to all boats measuring between 20 and 30 feet on the waterline.

The PC, measuring 31 feet, 10 inches overall and just 21 feet on the waterline, had a fixed, 2,400-pound lead keel, and displaced 5,000 pounds on a 6-foot, 8-inch beam, making it slim and fast.

In the same year as the Lipton Cup victory, four PCs from the San Diego YC took part in a six-week series of races in Honolulu against a fleet of four Herreshoff S-class boats, which were very similar in size and design. The four boats and their 12 sailors were taken to Hawaii by a U.S. Navy vessel, part of the congenial and mutually supportive arrangement that had existed between San Diego sailors and the Navy since the years of World War I, when local sailors donated their time and boats to the war effort.

──── PEARL HARBOR YACHT CLUB ────

After the Honolulu regatta, the sailors sold the entire fleet of PCs to the Pearl Harbor Yacht Club, leaving themselves boatless. They managed a return ride from another U.S. Navy vessel, this time aboard the battle cruiser *Chicago*, newly arrived in Honolulu after commissioning and sea trials. The *Chicago*'s next assignment was to attempt to break the record for a passage from Honolulu to San Francisco, which the vessel did. The *Chicago*, a flag vessel, had quarters on board for an admiral, but as the admiral was not going on this trip, the sailors were given his quarters and the status of "civilian observers."

With the PC's performance proven, the Kettenburg yard set about building them for an eager public, and from 1929 to the beginning of World War II, 35 of them hit the water. After the war, production began again, still in wood, and an additional 48 PCs were built, with the production finally stopping in 1952. There were 87 hull numbers assigned, but some of the assigned boats were never built.

With the onset of World War II, San Diego's harbor was closed with antisubmarine netting, and sailors found themselves limited to the bay area. They took to

sailing the diminutive 11-1/2-foot Rhodes-designed Penguin dinghy. Kettenburg responded to this by building 18 of them in 1942, finally going all out to military work after that.

After World War II, the Kettenburg yard produced the Pacific Coast Cruising Class, a 46-foot sloop. The PCC was every bit the boat the smaller PC was, and in 1946, a PCC from the San Diego YC won the Lipton Cup, finally bringing the cup back to the club's trophy chest after an absence of 15 years. The PCC was never as popular as its smaller cousin, though, and only 15 of them were built.

In San Francisco, there had been several local boats built, but they hadn't achieved the popularity of designs of the PC. An early attempt at a Bay one-design was done by the boat yard of Madden and Lewi, which engaged the services of F. C. Brewer. He drew the boat with a gaff rig, and the plans were sent to John Alden for a critique and, hopefully, Alden's imprimatur. Alden changed the rig to a bermudan, and Sam Crocker, who was working at the Alden yard in 1921, redrew the final lines.

THE BIRD BOAT

This became the Bird Boat, an inch short of 30 feet overall and 22 feet, 7 inches long at the waterline, and drawing 5 feet. The beam was narrow, at 7 feet, 8 inches, and as the Birds carried over 50 percent of their displacement in ballast, the boat would stand up to nearly anything the Bay had to offer.

While the design is marked in Alden's list of designs as his work, the owners of Birds will tell you the designer was really Brewer.

The Starlet, scaled down from the venerable Star class, was designed by San Diego YC member Joe Ruski for the use of the junior sailors. Their diminutive size can be seen by the standing crewmember on the center boat. *San Diego YC*

Kettenburg's Pacific Coast Cruising class, 46 feet long, was the big brother to the popular PC class. *San Diego YC*

The 46-foot Pacific Cruising Class was designed in 1946 by George Kettenburg of San Diego. The boat became popular all along the West Coast, by virtue of its combination of being a racing boat with comfortable cruising accommodations. The off-center companionway is typical of the Kettenburg designs. *Gossip*, shown here in 1956, won the Swiftsure Race in 1950 and placed seventh in the 1951 Honolulu Race, now the Transpac. It was owned by Phil Smith, commodore of the Seattle YC in 1951–1952. *Ken Ollar*

There were 25 hull numbers allotted, but only 21 of them were actually built, in a life span running from 1922 to 1934.

In 1930, local yards and sailors in the Bay were all feeling some of the effects of the Great Depression. What they needed was a small one-design boat that could be built for under a thousand dollars, smaller than the Bird, and even cheaper to build. At the Nunes Brothers yard in Sausalito there were many lengthy discussions on this subject until finally a model of the boat was carved out of a 6-by-6-inch piece of redwood. The conversations continued, this time refining the idea.

The boat that the Nunes brothers were debating was going to be an inexpensive boat. Against all advice, they put a transom-hung rudder on it, in the interests of saving money in construction costs and making the boat easier to repair. The overhanging stern was cut back for many of those same reasons.

The cockpit seats and the saloon seats were designed to sleep on, with the cockpit seats 5 feet, 6 inches long and the saloon seats an even 6 feet. The boat's overall design ethos was one of Spartan simplicity. The early 1930s were parlous times, and boatbuilders were feeling it worse than most, so they didn't want to take any risks. The boat (the design still didn't have a name) was just 23 feet long, and when it came time to launch the first one, the sails were of U.S. Army drill cloth.

The Nunes brothers made a keel mold from a large piece of redwood lying about the boat yard, and figured on a ballast of 1,000 pounds. By the time of the launch, the first boat still had no name. Among the local sailors of note attending this launch was the commodore of the San Francisco YC, who is reported to have said, "That is a bear of a boat," thereby giving the class its name.

There were a lot of changes made on hull number 1, including moving the mast aft and adding 250 pounds of ballast. Jigs were put together to get Bear assembly moving along smartly. Bears were built in good quantities; even during the war years of 1942–1946 there were 14 boats built. Construction had pretty much ceased in 1958, but there was one each built in 1975 and 1976. By then, 69 Bears had been built, of 70 assigned hull numbers. Unlike many other wood boats, in the case of the Bear it wasn't fiberglass that caused its demise, but the importation of wooden Folkboats from Europe at one-third the price.

A competitor to the Bear, although not a very successful one, was the Golden Gate One-Design, sometimes known as the Baby Bird. A naval architect named George Wayland, who worked at United Shipbuilding on the Bay, had been getting a lot of business, back in the 1930s, redrawing the rigging on boats whose gaff rig was being changed over to a bermudan. Much of this work came from sailors who couldn't afford to buy a new boat.

Wayland scaled down the Bird, taking it to just 24 feet, and reducing the rig in a proportionate fashion. The boat was bought in small quantities, but it came along

about the time of the Bear, and by most accounts the Bear was a better boat, so the Golden Gate never made it through the lengthy yachting hiatus of World War II.

In Seattle, the young sailors in the 1920s were sailing on what were known as "flatties," not built to any particular rule or design, but sharing in construction details such as being cross-planked on the hull and flat-bottomed, hence the name. They usually carried a short bowsprit, and despite the bowsprit, were gaff-rigged catboats.

In 1927, Seattle-area naval architect Ted Geary, known more for his larger boats, drew the first one-design flattie, keeping the basics of the hull shape, but changing the rig

The Bird boat, product of West Coast designer F. C. Brewer and revisions by John Alden, was built for the gusty winds of San Francisco Bay, with a high ballast ratio and relatively small sail area. *Mariah's Eyes*

(*previous page*) The recognizable Thunderbird, one of the most successful indigenous designs from the West Coast, has fleets all over the world. *Kelly O'Neill*

to a knockabout bermudan, improving the balance by adding power forward of the mast.

In January of the next year, members of the Seattle Yacht Club convened a meeting at the clubhouse, inviting anyone in Seattle interested in promoting junior sailing. Over seventy young sailors and their parents attended the

meeting, during which the plans from a dozen different designers were looked at and mulled over.

Eventually, Geary's flattie was selected, and that evening, as the wind was in their sails, so to speak, the group ordered 5 of them, to be built by N. J. Blanchard. Blanchard promised to deliver the first 10 boats for a cost of $150 each, $1,500 today, with any subsequent boats delivered for $200 each.

The flattie was sold as "an unsinkable sailboat provided for junior yachtsmen," and was the subject of much favorable press at the time, as well as considerable support from the Seattle YC. The flattie, which became the Geary 18, measures 18 feet 1 1/2 inches overall, with a beam of 5 feet, 5 1/2 inches and a displacement if 525 pounds. "Flattie" is perfectly descriptive of the zero-deadrise hull shape, which provides considerable form stability, and when the trapeze is used, allows the boat to be sailed on the turn of the bilge, reducing the wetted area. The sail area is 200 square feet, and class rules don't allow spinnakers, but do allow carrying a whisker pole for the jib.

The Star boat, that perennial favorite of sailors, has given rise to many similar boats, from the aforementioned Starlet to a Seattle design by Norman L. Blanchard called the Blanchard Knockabout, designed in 1934. The Blanchard family were boatbuilders, and involved in building Stars in those dark days early in the depression.

The Bear is a much-loved California native, designed, built, and sailed in the Bay area. The Bear fleet is still active on the Bay, sailing in the Master Mariner's Regatta every year. *Camembert* is hull number 57, launched in 1953. *Mariah's Eyes*

One of the lesser known sailboat classes of the Pacific Northwest was the Columbia River One Design, designed and built by Joe Dyer of the Astoria Ship Building Co. The CROD was built and sold as a racing boat during the early 1930s, and had its direct design antecedents in the working craft of the Columbia River. Fishermen there sailed a sprit-sail-rigged double-ender, most of them under 30 feet long. Dyer changed the stern to a conventional squared-off transom and gave his new boat a bermudan rig. The CROD shows its working-boat antecedents, with the easily built squared-off cabin and the wide side decks. In the background of this 1939 photograph is a Geary 18, with its crew working much harder to maintain the windward pace. *Ken Ollar*

Hearing many comments from sailors that the Star was a nice boat but "what it needs is a little cabin," Blanchard drew a set of lines on the shop floor, and when his son, Norman C. Blanchard, came to the shop the next day, he was detailed by his father to finish the design. The younger Blanchard stretched the Star out half a foot, put a small cabin on it, and the first Blanchard Knockabout was built directly form the lines on the shop floor, selling for $650 ($8,300 today). It used a keel identical to the Star and the name first chosen for it was the Star Knockabout, but the Star fleet sailors objected to any inference that the boat was a Star, so the

name was changed. To further confuse things, the boat is also known as the Senior Knockabout.

Sometimes, an enduring one-design seems to be almost a lucky accident, the fortuitous synchronicity of events where need meets fulfillment and everyone lives

translate the drawings into construction plans, and then he built the first Thunderbird in his waterfront shed.

The Thunderbird, 26 feet long and 20 feet long at the waterline, was an amazing success, right from the start. Much of the reason for its popularity lies with its

happily ever after. That was arguably the case with the Thunderbird class, developed in Seattle in 1958 as the result of a boat-design contest sponsored by the Douglas Fir Plywood Association.

Not surprisingly, the contest called for boats to be built of their material. The contest rules called for a boat that was "both a racing and a cruising boat," with the added requirement for it to sleep four and not require the skills of a seasoned salt to sail it. Finally, the boat had to be outboard powered and "outperform other sailboats in its class."

——— THE THUNDERBIRD ———

A young naval architect named Ben Seaborn entered the contest, and took his drawings and a cardboard model to Ed Hoppen, also of Seattle. It was Hoppen's job to

speed. The boat, made of plywood, is necessarily a hard-chine hull. Seaborn made the necessity very much a virtue by drawing the chines deep. As the boat heeled, the flat surface prevented leeway. Another factor was the keel, deep, with 5 feet of draft, and given a symmetrical hydrofoil shape.

Form stability was as important as ballasted stability. With a beam of 7 feet, 6 inches and the ballast ratio of 38 percent, the boat was often an embarrassment to the skippers of larger boats.

If there was to be one factor, though, that could be credited for the success of the Thunderbird, it had to be the remarkably low price. A set of plans, complete with building tips from Hoppen, was $2. Kits were a large part of the increasing fleet, and even today, nearly half the "new" Thunderbirds are home-built boats.

Although not the same scene as the East Coast as far as developing local boats, the West Coast, once the days of production boats began, would come into its own as a designer's haven. Designers and factories turned out boats that were desired and purchased by sailors from one coast to the other. But that's part of another, larger, national story; we will come back to the West Coast when the high-performance racers and well-designed cruisers from there began to be sailed by sailors nationwide. ✳

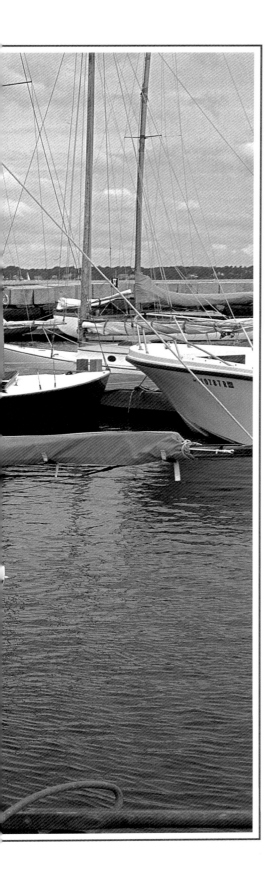

Building a Legacy

The Great American Shipyards

*T*he United States, separated from Europe by a vast ocean, began to build its own boats practically as soon as the first settlers arrived. These first boats were almost certainly built by the people who were going to sail them, namely, fishermen. If one wanted to be a fisherman, the first step was to build a boat. As the fishing industry grew, it eventually would support a separate industry, that of boatbuilding.

As outlined in other parts of this book, the working boat was the progenitor of all the early sailing designs, and with the development of a type of boat unique to the area, there came the beginnings of professional boatbuilders, people whose skills lay more with a saw and an adze than with a fishing net or a crab pot.

In the early years, these boatbuilders were small operations, located near their customers. But by the beginning of the twentieth century, they were starting to serve buyers who came from afar to obtain a boat by a particular designer. These early yards often combined the services of a designer and a builder, although yards such as Harry Nevins' and the Minneford yard, both in City Island, New York, were solely builders, working with such designers as Olin Stephens of Sparkman & Stephens, and Philip Rhodes.

Only three Herreshoff S-class boats were built at the Lawley yard, and *Lucky Pierre* is the sole survivor. This dockside photo affords a good opportunity to look at the cockpit of this beautiful daysailer. Note the long, generous coaming and the arched top to the cabin. *Paul Darling*

Brilliant, shown here with its original gaff mainsail, fitted topmast and square yard, made an Atlantic passage in 1932 from City Island to Plymouth, England, during which it averaged 200 miles a day for five days straight.

Rosenfeld Collection, Mystic Seaport

A mainstay of the yards on City Island, in the years when clubs such as the New York Yacht Club were specifying large classes such as the New York 30s, was supplying boats to New York YC members. The Nevins yard was especially suitable for the construction of larger boats, although things did slow down during the depression years. Olin Stephens, for one, considered the Nevins yard to be best in the country in the 1920s and 1930s.

The young Stephens set up a drafting table in the Nevins office in 1928, the year after he began his association with Drake Sparkman. He moved to his own office next door in 1929, after the new S&S partnership began to get commissions, which were built in yards besides Nevins'.

———————— THE NEVINS' BOATS ————————

In 1932 Nevins built the 61-foot, 6-inch S&S schooner *Brilliant*, designed with the goal of seagoing comfort and safety for owner Walter Barnum. The 56-foot cutter *Edlu*, and the 53-foot, 11-inch yawl

Stormy Weather, both S&S designs, followed in 1934, and were built side by side. To build three such landmark boats, noted everywhere for style, grace, quality of build, and a steady string of fast passages and racing successes, was truly the mark of a great yard.

In 1932, Nevins also built *Ayesha*, a Philip Rhodes–designed centerboard yawl that is thought of as the archetype of the shoal-draft offshore racer associated with Rhodes. The year of the boat's launch, it took third in class in the Bermuda Race. *Ayesha* measured 46 feet overall, 33 feet 2-1/2 inches on the waterline, 11 feet, 8-1/2 inches on the beam, and, with the shoal draft afforded by the centerboard, drew only 4 feet, 2-1/2 inches.

The design was so successful that *Ayesha*'s owner commissioned Rhodes in 1936 to build another, larger version, to be called *Alondra*. Eleven feet longer, *Alondra* had a 14-foot beam and drew 6 feet, 3-1/2 inches. Also built by Nevins, *Ayesha* and *Alondra* had forward galleys, typical of boats at that time with hired crew. Carleton Mitchell later bought *Alondra*, rechristened the boat *Caribee,* and raced it with great success until he commissioned the 38-foot S&S centerboarder *Finisterre* in 1954.

In 1936, the nation's finances were looking up a little and, by extension, so was business at Nevins. The New York 30s, designed and built at the Herreshoff yard in 1905, popular though they had been, were getting on in years, and the New York YC wanted a newer, larger boat. By 1936, only one 30, *Oriole*, was still registered in the New York fleet. Several boats measuring 32 feet on the waterline had been ordered by New York YC members, from an Olin Stephens design, and at the January 1936 general meeting of the club, Stephens' 32-footer was accepted after consideration of similarly sized boats offered by other designers. Stephens' boat became the New York 32.

The club ordered 20 of them, and the construction went to the Nevins yard. Measuring 45 feet, 4 inches overall, they were, of course, 32 feet on the waterline, 10 feet, 7 inches on the beam, and drew 6 feet, 6 inches. In

Stephens' autobiography, *All This and Sailing, Too,* he credits his partner, Drake Sparkman, as instrumental in S&S getting the commission. Sparkman worked closely with both Nevins and the Ratsey loft, which provided the sails, to deliver the boats as a complete package. The 32 was well built, planked with Philippine mahogany,

Alondra, here as *Caribee,* was a winning racer under the five-year ownership of Carleton Mitchell. Mitchell had the rig tuned and set up by Rod Stephens, which made the boat much faster to windward.

Rosenfeld Collection, Mystic Seaport

with frames of white oak, 1-5/8 inches wide on 80-inch centers, and bronze strappings. They were delivered for $11,000 each, or just over $136,000 today.

The year before, in 1935, Nevins had also built *Seven Seas,* a 12-meter designed by Clinton Crane. In 1939 the yard built another 12-meter, commissioned by Harold Vanderbilt and designed by Stephens. This boat was called *Vim,* the first 12-meter to carry an aluminum mast. In 1949, Nevins built the 73-foot yawl, *Bolero,* designed by Stephens under the CCA rule. *Bolero* set the course record for the Bermuda Race in 1956, and was one of the first boats on which stresses were measured. When Rod Stephens attached a strain gauge to the genoa sheets, he discovered that the big headsail had a pull of over two tons. This discovery led to the development of stronger winches and better line.

Nineteen thiry-nine was also the year that Nevins built the Rhodes 27, an even dozen of them, under commission by the Fire Island Yacht Club. Named for the waterline length, the boats measured 39 feet, 2 inches overall, with a beam of 9 feet, 8 inches and a draft of 5 feet, 10 inches. The boat was so successful that after the first fleet was built for the Fire Island YC, the design was made available to the general public as a one-design, and built on the Great Lakes and the West Coast. Rigged as a three-quarter fractional sloop, the Rhodes 27 carried 635 square feet of sail.

Nevins also built the famous 54-foot yawl, *Stormy Weather,* Olin's favorite boat by most accounts. The excellence of its design was apparent even out of the water. In the winter of 1935, for example, John Alden was strolling through the Nevins yard, when he saw *Stormy,* with only its hull visible under the tarpaulin covering the boat for the winter.

"A better design would be impossible to achieve," said Alden, whose role as America's preeminent yacht designer was on the wane with the shift to bermudan rigs on sloops, cutters, ketches, and yawls, and schooners, although beloved, now becoming scarce on the launching ways.

In 1937, Nevins built an Alden boat, the third one named *Zaida,* for George Ratsey. *Zaida* was 57 feet, 5 inches on deck and launched as a cutter, but was rerigged as a yawl a year after. During World War II, the boat was used in antisubmarine patrols off the Atlantic coast, and in a violent midwinter storm, all 1,834 square feet of sail were blown out. After drifting for 23 days, *Zaida* was finally rescued and towed home, arriving on Christmas Eve, by coincidence the same night that George Ratsey died at his home.

During the years of World War II, the Nevins yard changed hands and many key personnel left, including the yard manager. The yard maintained its name, but Henry Nevins was no longer in charge.

──────── HERRESHOFF BOATS ────────

The Herreshoff yard in Bristol, Rhode Island, was a yard that could both design and build. An established family business, it had been building boats since 1863. By the turn of the twentieth century, Herreshoff Manufacturing Company employed around 200 people, who made 50 cents an hour, on average, or slightly more than 10 dollars an hour today. At the time, the workers considered it to be a fair wage, and the company was known for its speed of construction as well as its quality.

Herreshoff was what might today be called a "one-stop boat yard," making sails, boats, masts, hardware—even the paint—on-site. It could, and did, work with incredible dispatch. In one storied incident, the owner of a New York 30 broke a spar in a race and needed another made for the next race. In 24 hours of nonstop labor, the spar was finished and the boat entered the race.

The Herreshoff yard practically had a monopoly on the making of large cross-cut sails (invented by Nat Herreshoff, with the seams running at right angles to the leech). In 1901, the owners of the two America's Cup boats that were in close contention for the honor of defending the Cup both came to Herreshoff for a new suit of sails. One of the boats, *Constitution*, was a Herreshoff design, and operated by a syndicate of well-off sailors. J. P and E. D.

Morgan owned the other boat, *Columbia*, sailors with even more impeccable finances. There was only time to make one set of sails, and Herreshoff decided to make them for his design, *Constitution*. Thus, a few years later, the English sailmaker Ratsey came to City Island to set up shop, at the tacit encouragement of J. P. Morgan.

Stormy Weather was built in 1934 for the express purpose of ocean racing, which she did exceedingly well. The delivered price was exactly to contract, $20,000 ($257,000 today), and even by the standards of the day, a bargain. Olin Stephens has said a boat like built today would "comeinto the $800,000-dollar-range." *Stormy Weather* has recently been restored and is now sailing in the Mediterranean.

Rosenfeld Collection, Mystic, Connecticut

Nathanael Herreshoff was practically the house designer for members of the New York YC, so much so that in 1902 he was voted in as an honorary member. The Seawanhaka Corinthian YC followed suit a few years later. Besides his design work, he was honored for his formulation of the Universal Rule and his work in the defense of the America's Cup. Being elected a permanent honorary member at the New York YC was a distinction not freely given; other honorary members at the time included the king of England, the prince of Wales, Germany's Kaiser, and Sir Thomas Lipton.

In 1904, the New York YC began to talk with Nat Herreshoff about a new design, this one to be 30 feet on the waterline. By the spring of 1905, 18 had been built, at a cost of $4,000 apiece, fully outfitted with everything from sails to bed linens to dishes. To put that amount in perspective, that is nearly $78,000 today.

A big order like that, for identical boats, was money in the bank for the Herreshoff yard, and while a production line was set up to turn them out quickly, work still proceeded on the many other commissions at the yard, including steam yachts and many smaller vessels. So active was the motor yacht business that the income from that aspect of his business represented fully half of the company's income.

In 1912, the yard had another major commission, again from the New York YC, this one to build the New York 50s. Measuring 72 feet overall and drawing 9 feet, they were the largest class ever of big one-design boats, with nine of them ordered and built in the winter of 1912–1913. They were delivered for a total cost of $17,000 including sails, equal to slightly more than $294,000 in 2000 dollars. Their first race was on May 24, 1913, off Glen Cove, New York.

While the yard was engaged in production boats, such was the scale of the business at the time that they still took on huge individual commissions. One of the best examples of this was the steel schooner, *Katoura,* measuring 162 feet overall, begun the winter after the New York 50s were completed.

Katoura was so big it took up an entire workshop, and weighed so much, 313 tons, that for fear the ways would not handle the weight, a quarter of the ballast was to be placed inside after launch in the form of specially cast lead blocks. The foremast was the hollow steel

The author participated in the 1991 Fastnet Race on board *Stormy Weather,* which finished 50th overall and was awarded the Iolaire Block for being the oldest boat in the race.

Greg Jones

main mast salvaged from *Constitution* and the main was the mainmast of *Reliance,* both purchased when the boats were broken up for salvage. Built to race, *Katoura* even had a folding propeller.

The next big order for boats from the New York YC was for that club's 40s. The first order was for 12 boats, built over the winter of 1915–1916, with two more made in 1926. Measuring 72 feet overall, drawing 9 feet, 9 inches, they were slender, in the manner of the time, with a beam-to-length ratio of just over 1:4, and more than adequately powered with a big gaff main, a sprit-rigged topsail, and a clubfooted jib with a jib topsail. Later, some of them were rerigged as bermudan yawls, and in 1924 and 1928, rerigged 40s won the Newport–Bermuda Race.

By then, the Herreshoff Manufacturing Co. had begun to fall on hard times. Run by a consortium of businessmen since 1915, the company was put for up auction in 1924, and while the purchaser maintained the name Herreshoff Manufacturing Co., from that day onward Cap'n Nat was, in effect, a contract designer—in many cases for the company that still bore his name but with which he had no other connection.

The Herreshoff yard continued to build yachts, many of them, including three of the big J-class boats and another *Katoura*, this one a 112-foot- overall steel yacht built to the International Rule, for Robert Tod, who had commissioned the earlier, 162-foot *Katoura*. The later *Katoura* was a Starling Burgess design.

In 1930, the yard built two Cup boats, *Enterprise* and *Weetamoe*, but when the 1936 contract for the New York 32 was awarded, it went to the Nevins yard. During World War II, the company survived on military contracts, but by 1945, the Herreshoff Manufacturing Co. was no more.

— The Minneford Yard —
Right next door to the Nevis yard and Olin Stephens was the Minneford yard, owned by H. S. Sayers. Sayers was not a boatbuilder at all, but was what today would be termed a real-estate developer, in City Island and the Bronx. His two sons, Henry and Dick, ran the yard.

The first S&S design capable of offshore sailing was the 30-foot sloop *Kalmia*. This design was built as a racing boat and earned immediate success, taking first in its initial contest, the Gibson Island Race of 1929. The designer and the rest of the Stephens family raced *Kalmia* on its maiden voyage, and Sayers was so impressed with the boat, he had his yard build him a larger version for his personal use. This larger boat, incidentally, was the first commission taken at S&S's new office.

Kalmia marked the beginning of a long and productive relationship between S&S and Minneford's, ending with the construction of the Cup defender *Freedom* in 1979.

In the winter of 1929–1930 Minneford built *Tidal Wave*, a Philip Rhodes double-ended ketch measuring 32 feet, 4 inches overall, and 31 feet on the waterline on an 11-foot beam, drawing 5 feet. *Tidal Wave* was lightly

ballasted, with a ballast ratio of only 28 percent, but still stood up to the wind because of the flaring topsides and its beam-to-length ratio of 2.94. *Tidal Wave* was designed in 1927 and built for Samuel Wetherill, an associate editor at *Yachting* magazine, who worked closely with Rhodes in getting exactly the boat he wanted.

In 1930 Minneford built *Dorade*, one of Stephens' most famous boats, with the watertight ventilation boxes on the topsides that pay tribute to the boat with every mention of a dorade box. *Dorade*, a 52-foot ketch, was commissioned by Olin Stephen's father, Olin Sr., and built for the astonishing price of $28,000 1930 dollars, equal to $288,000 today—a truly exceptional value for a boat that has won, at one time or another, virtually every

Coming back from the Fastnet Rock, *Stormy* sailed through winds strong enough to knock the stove off its gimbals. The wind speed was 40 knots, with a double-reefed main and the mizzen struck. Of all of the photographs taken on the race, there are only two left. The British Royal Mail unapologetically lost the rest. *Greg Jones*

The Herreshoff 12-1/2 was a mainstay of the Herreshoff yard. Over the winter of 1914–1915, 20 of them were built, for the delivered price of $420 ($7,100 today). This is *Bull Head*, hull number 3, at a junior race in 1926. *Rosenfeld collection, Mystic, Connecticut*

111

major ocean race. The year of its launch, 1930, *Dorade* took second in Class B in the Bermuda Race, and the next year, with Olin Senior and Olin Junior and Rod Stephens aboard, won the Newport, Rhode Island, to Plymouth, England, Transatlantic, finishing two days ahead of the next boat. *Dorade* followed that triumph with a win in the 1931 Fastnet Race. When the Stephens family returned to New York City, they were given a ticker-tape parade down Broadway, an unprecedented event for sailors.

It would be difficult to follow a success the magnitude of *Dorade*, but the next year, Minneford built *Narwhal*, another Rhodes double-ender, for Sayers. Referred to by Rhodes on the plans as a "development of the *Tidal Wave* type," *Narwhal* was identical in measurement to *Tidal Wave* except for slightly greater length—at 39 feet, 11 inches, just over 7 feet longer. This was accomplished by drawing out *Narwhal's* plumb bow. *Narwhal* was cutter-rigged, with nearly 200 additional square feet of sail at 864 square feet, and was known as a fast boat.

In the 1930s, yards and designers were struggling, with the depression affecting every aspect of boatbuilding.

Katoura was said by L. Francis Herreshoff himself to be the finest all-round yacht ever built by Herreshoff Manufacturing Co. In this 1914 photo, Katoura is to the left and Resolute, the Herreshoff-designed America's Cup defender, is center.

Herreshoff Marine Museum

Commercial work continued at a reduced pace, but commissions for bigger yachts had slowed to a trickle. The industry responded by designing smaller, less expensive boats. The design firm of Cox & Stevens took on Philip Rhodes to produce stock designs for yachtsmen who wanted a boat, but were no longer as flush as they had been. In 1935, in conjunction with the Minneford yard, Rhodes designed the Minneford Cutter, a transom-sterned vessel with a full keel, exhibiting a good deal of drag and terminating in an attached, transom-hung rudder nearly as deep as the keel.

Working together closely, Rhodes and the yard produced a boat that was as inexpensive as possible to build, but maintained strength and a sweet shape. Deep, with an arched cabintop, the 32-foot, 9-inch-overall Minneford Cutter had 6 feet of headroom. With all the drag to the keel setting the center of lateral resistance quite far aft, the mainsail was big, so big the boat had running backstays. The big main contributed to the overall sail area of 738 square feet.

In 1937, Minneford built the 41-foot yawl *Golden Eye*, another Rhodes design, reviewed in *Rudder* the same year. Although not designed as a racing boat, *Golden Eye* still went out in its first year and took Class B honors at the Gibson Island–New London Race.

In 1939, S&S released the 23-foot sloop *Raceabout*, a one-design. This boat is not to be confused with the Raceabout class in Marblehead, an offshoot of the famous Knockabouts of the early twentieth century.

The Lawley Yard

The George Lawley & Sons yard was founded in 1866, 12 years before the Herreshoff yard, with which it competed boat-to-boat. The yard began in Scituate, Massachusetts, moving across the harbor to Neponset, Massachusetts, in 1911. Lawley built more small boats and tenders than it did large yachts, compiling a record of 1,890 boats less than 30 feet long, and more than 1,100 larger boats.

Both George and Fred Lawley designed boats as well, including the Lawley 15, one of the better known of their designs, of which 20 were built in 1938. Fred Lawley designed some large schooners in the early part of the twentieth century, ranging from 64 to 84 feet in length, and in 1903, designed a 73-foot yawl.

The yard in its heyday was immense. It filled a peninsula into the harbor, with two large three-story buildings at the entrance and eight buildings behind them. The list of designers the Lawleys worked with is practically a who's who of yacht design: John Alden, Edward Burgess, Sam Crocker, Bowdoin B. Crowninshield, Nathanael and L. Francis Herreshoff, Walter McInnis, and Olin Stephens, among others.

Over the winter of 1926–1927, *Barbette*, a Sam Crocker yawl measuring 50 feet, 9 inches overall, was built at Lawley's for a member of the Bayview (Detroit) Yacht Club. *Barbette* carried 1,502 square feet of sail, driving a displacement of 41,000 pounds, with a moderate beam of 14 feet. Full-keeled, in the manner of

In their first season, the 50s took up racing seriously. Here, in one of the first races of that season, the fleet heads off to windward at the start. *Rosenfeld collection, Mystic, Connecticut*

Crocker's boats, it drew an even 5 feet. The boat's heavy displacement-to-length ratio made it a good sea boat, and there was enough sail, with a sail area-to-displacement ratio of 20.3, to keep it going. The boat won the Detroit–Macinac Race in 1927 and 1929, and is still the subject of debate in the Bayview Yacht Club for its victory in the club's annual All Night Race, in which, by the recorded time, *Barbette* averaged over 10 knots in a 68-mile race.

In 1936, Lawley launched *Rubaiyat* (for an owner named Nathaniel Rubinkam), a cutter measuring 43 feet, 2 inches overall, 30 feet, 4 inches on the waterline, with a relatively narrow beam of 10 feet, 8 inches. *Rubaiyat* drew 6 feet, and was a successful racer from its first days. The boat won the Chicago–Macinac Race in 1936 and 1937. The 1937 win was all the more remarkable as it was the race known as the Hard Blow of 1937. Only 8 of 42 starting boats finished, in winds so serious the event ranks as only one of four, in more than a century's worth of Mac races, to have been run in full-gale conditions.

The Weekender, designed by Olin Stephens in 1937, was a response to the times; ordinary sailors wanted a boat they could enjoy with the same exuberance as those wealthier sailors with large, custom-designed boats. The Weekender was the answer, 35 feet overall on a waterline of 27 feet. Measuring 9 feet, 6 inches on the beam, drawing 5 feet, 7 inches with a sail area of 562 square feet, Stephens managed to design a boat that had 6 feet, 2 inches of headroom with cockpits 6-1/2 feet long and berths of 6 feet, 3 inches.

The Weekenders were fast, with victories in the Chicago–Mac inac race and the American Yacht Club Cruise. Thirty-seven of them were built in their first two seasons, 17 of them by Lawley.

The Q-class boats, built to the Universal Rule, first showed up in Marblehead around 1909. The Qs,

roughly comparable to the 8-meter class, were built to a formula developed by Nat Herreshoff in 1903, at first called the Herreshoff Rule, but soon called the Universal Rule. Q-class boats had lengths of roughly 50 feet, and the Lawley yard built at least six of them between 1923 and 1939. Q-12, designed by Nat Herreshoff, was launched in 1928, and named *Nor'easter V*. Long, lean, and deep, *Nor'easter* is 50 feet overall, has an 8-foot beam, and draws nearly 7 feet. The boat started its racing career at the Eastern Yacht Club in Marblehead, but these days, with its sister ship *Questa*, is a charter vessel in, of all places, Flathead Lake, Montana.

CAPE COD BOATS

Lawley's fortunes began to ebb in the late 1930s. During World War II Lawley had naval contracts, and

apparently had thoughts of changing direction; in 1941, the company sold the entire small boat department to the Cape Cod Shipbuilding Company. Yet neither the military contracts nor the cash from the sale of the bigger part of the company was enough. Finally, in 1945, the same year that its long-time rival the Herreshoff Manufacturing Co. closed, George Lawley & Sons went out of business.

Cape Cod Shipbuilding Co. of Wareham, Massachusetts, began as the Cape Cod Power Dory Company in 1899, changing its name in 1919 to its present one, concurrent with its moving to the other side of the bay to avoid being shut off from the sea by the construction of the Narrows Bridge.

Started by brothers Myron and Charles Gurney, with the latter doing the designing and drafting, the yard's first major success was the Cape Cod Knockabout, discussed earlier. Frugality was the order of the day, and the windows and doors of the new premises were made from salvaged materials obtained from buildings being torn down in the center of town. They took in trees, and put out boats, storing the timber in a separate building from the boats to limit damages in the event of a fire.

During the early years the company produced mostly pleasure craft, with a few commercial boats built as opportunities arose. Boats were built upside down, speeding the process, and the company, in its official history, boasts that "not a scrap [of wood] went to waste," one of the advantages of doing their own milling.

In 1939, Les Goodwin purchased the business. Goodwin formerly owned the Undercliff Boat Works in New Jersey, and also was a dealer for Cape Cod's boats. With the death of Charles Gurney, and the company management taken over by G. S. Williams, Cape Cod's finances began to reflect poor management. Goodwin bought the yard, now down to one employee, a rigger named Jack Daphney.

Rubaiyat, its fame ensured by winning one of the stormiest Chicago–Mackinac races in history, is still sailing, in the waters of southern California. *John Alden, Inc*

Goodwin changed the whole philosophy of the company. Rather than build only boats designed in-house, he sought the best designers, purchased those designs, and produced desirable boats. The first such boats built under Goodwin were the Rhodes 18 and the S&S Mercury.

Rhodes designed the 18 in 1938 for use as a junior trainer by the Stamford (Connecticut) Yacht Club. The 18-foot-overall boats came as either centerboard or keelboats, with the keel version displacing 950 pounds and the centerboarder 800. Fractionally rigged, carrying 162 square feet of main and jib, plus a 197 square-foot spinnaker, the Rhodes 18 was a hot boat. The lighter centerboard version was more popular, and over 700 keel and centerboarders were built, becoming popular after Cape Cod began to make the design

available as a one-design. In 1948, Cape Cod, which was in the forefront of the fiberglass revolution, began to make the 18 in fiberglass.

The S&S Mercury, called the Cape Cod Mercury (to avoid confusion with the larger, Ernest Nunes–designed Mercury that appeared at about the same time), was 15 feet, 3 inches overall, 11 feet, 10 inches on the waterline, and like the Rhodes came as a keel or centerboard boat. It was a lighter boat, as might be expected, with the keel version displacing 730 pounds and the centerboard 420.

Cape Cod sold 200 wooden Mercuries between 1940 and 1952, and then adapted the design for fiberglass. The first 10 fiberglass Mercuries went to Community Boating Inc., in Boston, where they are still sailing.

Cape Cod's program of acquiring designs continued. As noted above, the spirit of the fine small boats produced at Lawley lived on at Cape Cod Shipbuilding, and in 1947, Cape Cod obtained exclusive rights to all Herreshoff designs under 30 feet. Some of the designs were kept in-house to build boats to them, while the rest were taken to the Massachusetts Institute of Technology for restoration.

Soon after acquiring the Herreshoff plans, Cape Cod built 35 of the 12-1/2-foot Bullseyes in wood, and then in 1950 began to make the Fisher Island 12-1/2 in fiberglass. This version of Cap'n Nat's Bullseye (also called, variously, the Doughdish, Buzzards Bay Class, and Narragansett Bay Class) was designed by him for the Fisher Island fleet, and among other changes had a tiller that went over the stern, rather than through it in the fashion of the Bullseye. The Fisher Island 12-1/2 was considered to be more seaworthy, and, in fiberglass, became known as the Cape Cod Bullseye. In the first decade of the Cape Cod Bullseye, the yard sold more than one a week, compared to nearly two a week of the larger Mercury.

The end of the Cape Cod shipbuilding story is far more upbeat than that of the preceding yards. It is in business today, still concentrating on small boats. During the lifetime of founder Charles Gurney, the yard built more than 16,000 boats, most of them in the 12- to 20-foot range, and that tradition continues today.

OTHER BOAT YARDS

The boat yards whose histories are detailed here are, by necessity, only a small sampling, a selection of the more prominent and more historically interesting yards from among many, many more. The others have been omitted because only a limited number can be covered properly within the confines of a single volume. Yet these other yards, collectively, give a sense for the vastness of this once diverse and proud industry. They include the following: Baltzer (maker of mostly in-house-designed boats); Bath Iron Works (which, although known more for its naval vessels, made a wide variety of pleasure craft as well); Carl Beetle (of Beetle Cat fame, whose yard also made, in 1939, a Sam Crocker New Bedford 35 and other large boats); Dauntless (which made a number of Alden boats); Goudy & Stephens (also maker of

The 45-foot sloop *Lark* was designed by John Alden in 1932 and built the same year at the Lawley yard. *Lark* is Alden Design Number 531. *Paul Darling*

The Herreshoff-designed
Q-class *Nor'easter* (*in
foreground*), after years as a
saltwater racing boat, now
charters in the mountains
of Montana, along with its
sister ship *Questa*, designed
by L. Francis Herreshoff in
1929. *Nor'easter* was built
at the Lawley yard in 1928,
one of only seven Q-class
built there. *Jeffrey Goodman*

a number of Alden designs, as well as Crocker designs); Henry R. Hinckley Company; Hodgdon Brothers (maker of boats by William Hand Jr., B. B. Crowninshield, Alden, S&S, Bowes & Mower, and others); Huntington Manufacturing Company (Crowninshield, Charles Mower, and in-house-designed boats); Robert Jacob (Cox & Stevens, Mower, Hand, S&S, Francis Sweisguth, Louis Kromholz, and others); Simms Brothers (Crocker, S&S, Alberg, K. Aage Nielsen, and others); Kretzer Boat Works (S&S, Rhodes, Cox & Stevens, Mower, and others); Luders Marine (many in-house designs by Alfred Luders Jr., including the line of Sea Sprites, except for the 23, by Carl Alberg); Milton Boat Works (Mower, Alden, R. R. Crosby, and others); Mystic Shipyard (Alden, Rhodes, and others); Oxford Shipyards, Inc. (S&S, Frederick Geiger, and others); the F. F. Pendelton yard (many Alden boats, some S&S, and others); Quincy Adams Yacht Yard (Alden, S&S, L. Francis Herreshoff, Fred Goeller Jr., and others); Read Brothers (mostly in-house designs); Willis Reid (Crocker, C. R. Snow, Furnans Yacht Agency, and others); Smith & Williams (mostly J. Murray Watts, with a 75-foot Mower schooner in 1921); W. F. Stone (Bowes & Mower, Crowninshield, and others); Wilmington Boat Works (Hand, S&S, Rhodes, and others); and Woodnutt & Company.

Sadly, the above list is very nearly an obituary of American boatbuilding. Most of the companies listed no longer exist. Some have been gone for years; others, including Luders Marine, which went out of business in 1968, are of more recent departure. Still other yards, such as Bath Iron Works, remain in business, but not the yacht business, while others, like

Hinckley Company, are alive and well and still building yachts. No longer does nearly every coastal town have a boat yard where local sailors have boats built. There are now boat dealers in every town, selling boats very much like the boats being sold in the next town down the coast. Boats are more available than ever before, however, perhaps because of the very same causes that eliminated the small boat yards: large companies with highly organized distribution networks and mass-production techniques. ✳

The Cape Cod Catboat was a style developed by working fishermen, with low freeboard, an easily tended rig, and perfected by the Crosby family of boatbuilders. The Crosbys, of Osterville, Massachusetts, built their family's reputation on the design and building of catboats, at one time operating five separate yards on the Osterville seafront. The photograph is dated 1941, but the boat is almost assuredly older.

Mystic Seaport, Rosenfeld collection, Mystic, Connecticut. Image acquired in honor of Hudson H. Bubar

Weathering the Storm

The Sailboat Industry in the Great Depression

*W*hen the stock market crashed on October 14, 1929, it brought down more than the price of shares. The business of making pleasure boats changed dramatically. Many boatbuilders simply disappeared, while others reduced both their work force and the size of boats they built. To designers, the change in the economic tides was a design challenge: how could they design a boat sailors would enjoy that wouldn't exceed their financial limits?

The S&S Weekender is an example of a boat built for the finances of the times, even though the Great Depression's leanest period was past when it came out in 1937. The design was successful, not only in the number of boats built, but in the most sincere form of flattery: imitation. (See chapter 6 for more on the Weekender.)

In 1937, John Alden drew the Coastwise Cruiser, which, although very different in design, was done with the idea of providing an affordable boat. The Coastwise Cruiser measured 36

The Fisher Island 31 is one of Herreshoff's loveliest boats but was a victim of the Great Depression, replaced by the smaller Fisher Island 23. *Cirrus*, shown here, races in the area near Newport, Rhode Island. The last Fisher Island 31 was launched in 1930, aptly named *Last Straw*. The boat is 44 feet overall, with 31 feet on the waterline, has a 10-foot, 7-inch beam, and draws 6-foot, 1-inch. Exceptionally seaworthy boats, the Fisher Island 31 *Patapsco II* took its owners around the world in the mid-1960s. *Alison Langley*

feet, 5 inches overall and was an inch less than 26 feet on the waterline. With a beam of 9 feet, 9 inches and a draft of 5 feet, 3 inches, it was certainly similar to the S&S Weekender, but the Alden boat bore his stamp, with a narrow, graceful, overhanging stern and a sheer line that added to the good looks.

Rigged originally as a three-quarter fractional cutter, carrying 585 square feet of sail, some of the Coastwise Cruisers had bowsprits and were delivered as masthead cutters. With a self-tending headsail on both models and standing backstays, Alden's boat was easy to handle. Its full keel, with a barely perceptible amount of drag to it, would keep the boat level when leaned against a dock to receive a new coat of bottom paint between tides.

The Coastwise Cruiser sold for $6,500 in 1938, just over $79,000 today. There were a number of clever design solutions inincorporated to make this 36-footer capable of taking four people out in reasonable comfort. In the days before electronics, the chart table was vital, but it took up a lot of room—space out of proportion to the regularity of use, but vital for the safety of the boat. Alden designed a folding chart table that extended out over the port settee, freeing the space when the crew was not plotting navigation.

The forward V-berth could be shut off from the saloon by the door to the clothes locker, which when fully opened closed just as nicely against the forward bulkhead. An enclosed head and a galley with a sink to starboard and the stove to port might have kept the cook busy changing sides, but it was a good solution to the problem of space on a small boat.

Tankage was considerable. Two 20-gallon fuel tanks, below and on either side of the cockpit, provided a good fuel supply; the only glitch in the tankage arrangement was the

40-gallon water tank, which when full put 320 pounds of weight well outboard to starboard. The engine was set slightly off to port to counteract this, but the boat still had a slight list to starboard with a full tank.

The depression was about at its worst in 1932 and 1933. In 1932 Seawanhaka Corinthian Yacht Club was only able to gather four of the New York 30s on the starting line for the spring and fall regattas, and they were the largest boats raced that year. In 1933, the club began to award pennants instead of cups, "as an economy in this year of business depression," according to the club history. The practice continued until 1937, and

Lucky Star, hull number 1 of Alden's Coastwise Cruiser class, was wrecked in a hurricane in 1938, shortly after being launched. It was rebuilt by the owner, but so extensively modified in the process that the boat was no longer eligible to participate in the very active class association races on Long Island Sound. The photograph dates from 1941; note the large wartime registration numbers on the bow.

Rosenfeld collection, Mystic, Connecticut

in the S-class, the winners took to flying their trophy pennants from the spreaders.

The early 1930s were a good time to build an inexpensive boat. In 1931, the economy was spiraling downward, and the effects were being felt everywhere. Keeping a boat in a slip in a marina was out of the question for many sailors, but the boat trailer, by then relatively well developed, provided an alternative. Boat trailers increased in popularity with the growth of scow racing in the inland lakes: boats regularly competed in different lakes, and the only way to take one's boat to the host club's lake was to pull it behind a car.

In March 1931 Florida's West Coast Racing Association held one of their usual meetings, and a hot topic at this meeting was the delegates' expressed desire for a small boat that could be transported by trailer. They decided to call the boat concept the Trailer class. Attending this meeting was William F. Crosby, of *Rudder* magazine; he claimed he could design a boat that would fit the bill precisely.

Crosby set to work and by July printed a set of plans for a Trailer-class dinghy in that month's issue of *Rudder*. The magazine designated the boat the Snipe. *Rudder* named all boats introduced by the magazine after sea birds, in honor of *Rudder* editor Tom Fleming Day's self-designed 25-foot yawl, *Sea Bird*. The magazine credited Crosby for the plans and that issue was soon sold out, bought up by sailors eager to try their hand at

Snipes are uncomplicated, with a minimum of strings to pull, and very well-balanced. Even working to windward, there is only a small amount of weather helm. Note the simplified vang. *Rosenfeld Collection, Mystic, Connecticut*

making a boat that Crosby promised could be built at home for under $100 ($1,100 in 2000 dollars).

THE SNIPE

The Snipe was a hard-chine design, lending itself well to home construction. The first boats were plank-built, with a switch to plywood as it became affordable and as better glues were developed. The length, 15 feet, 6 inches, was established so it could be built using standard 16-foot planks.

The hull has a fairly steep angled, reversed, flat transom and an evenly radiused bow, giving it a waterline of 13 feet, 6 inches. It was designed to be relatively beamy, at 5 feet, simple to rig, and, with the original rig measuring only 100 square feet, easy to sail.

Those early Snipes weighed 425 pounds and could even be carried on the roof of a car, for those sailors who lacked a trailer but had the muscle to hoist it into place.

A 14-year-old boy from Pass Christian, Mississippi, named Jimmy Brown, and his father built hull number

home-built Snipes began to show up at races sponsored by local clubs, and by the end of that summer several of the large national racing associations had recognized the class by giving Snipes their own starts.

In November 1932, a Dallas, Texas, sailor named Hub E. Isaacks formed the Snipe Class International Racing Association (SCIRA), and not a minute too soon. By the end of 1932 there were 250 boats registered, and the class went international in March of 1933 when a fleet formed in Dover, England.

Those first Snipes had, as noted, a fairly modest sail plan of 100 square feet, with a 100 percent working jib. The jib was increased to 150 percent in 1932, giving the Snipe a total sail area of 116 square feet, and some years later the mainsail was increased in size to yield 128 square feet. From the beginning it was designed as a non–spinnaker class, supplying instead a whisker pole to boom out the jib on a run.

Crosby had truly designed a winner. By July 1936 the Snipe class was the world's largest racing class, with fleets literally worldwide. The first "world championship"

(*opposite*) The action on a Snipe can be some of wettest and wildest in the world of dinghy sailing. Although this is a state-of-the-art Snipe, it is interesting to compare it with the older models. *Onne van der Wal*

The Columbia River One Design came from an existing working-boat design; with money short in the 1930s, Joe Dyer adapted the lines of a fishing boat, the double-ended Columbia River gillnetter. *Ken Ollar*

1. Crosby couldn't have asked for a first boat that more nearly exemplified his intentions behind the design.

Rudder magazine began to receive letters from successful builders as early as September 1931. Soon there were so many owners that *Rudder* began to issue hull numbers.

Garages and driveways all around the country had Snipes sitting in them: by May 1932 there were 150 boats on *Rudder*'s list. Those

was held in 1934, but it was worldwide in name only, like baseball's World Series in which just American teams competed.

The history of the Snipe, propelled onto the stage by the economics of the 1930s, deserves some continuation, even if the story takes us past the decade of its founding. In 1946, the Snipe world championship merited the name. Sailors from Brazil, Newfoundland, Portugal, and Switzerland joined their American counterparts on Lake Chautauqua, New York, and it was a watershed event for the class.

The trophy for the American Snipe champion was the Hub Isaacks Trophy, named for the founder of the SCIRA. Snipe commodore Charles Heinzerling decided to design a new trophy for the American champion, freeing the Isaacks trophy to be awarded at the international level.

Competing at that first international Snipe regatta was Dr. Martin Dupan of Switzerland. He was impressed with the Lake Chautauqua event and began to campaign to have the next world championship held on his home waters of Lake Geneva, Switzerland.

In Wichita, Kansas, a sailor named Ted Wells had built a Snipe; the only water he had to sail on was a pond made to provide water for the steam engines of the Santa Fe railroad. Wells, probably very skilled in short-tacking drills, took his skills to Lake Geneva in 1947 and brought home the Isaacks Cup, taking first place in a Snipe racing fleet of boats from 13 countries.

Rudder magazine had been selling the plans to Snipes since the day that July 1931 issue sold out, but in 1948 it sold them to SCIRA. In 1954 it became SCIRA, Inc., and Snipes were finally recognized as an international class by the International Yacht Racing Union in 1958.

Huge fleets crowding the starting line are a common sight at Lightning regattas, sharpening the sailors' skills.

By 1963, there were 14,700 Snipes, racing in 500 fleets in 30 countries, and in the early 1970s, SCIRA made the biggest single change in the class' history, when the minimum weight of a Snipe was reduced from Crosby's original 425 pounds to 381 pounds.

The year following the Snipe's introduction, 1932, the Comet class began, a story covered in chapter 3. The Comet met with similar success, albeit with smaller numbers than the easily built Snipe.

Those designers and builders that adapted to the times were less affected by the depression than most. Olin Stephens recalls in his autobiography, *All This and Sailing, Too*, that his office, neighbor to the Nevins and the Minneford yards, was able to work with those two yards more than ever because the aspect of the yards' business pertaining to building larger boats had declined and they "were available to build our smaller boats . . . I was less aware of the Depression than most."

"Smaller," especially in the business of custom yachts, is a relative term, of course, and it was the 1930s that saw the design and construction of such wonderful boats as *Dorade*, *Brilliant*, and *Stormy Weather*, covered in other parts of this book.

There were, of course, some people whose fortunes were seemingly not bothered by the problems of Wall Street. Edward F. Hutton's four-masted bark, *Hussar* (later *Sea Cloud*), joined the member's fleet of the New York YC in 1931, all 316 feet of it, with a crew of 70. The New York YC history records that Hutton urged "other owners of large yachts to continue to keep them in commission during the business depression in order to provide employment and stimulate business concerns that supplied and maintained the vessel." The records note that "many owners did not follow his example."

Indeed, as the decade wore on, even the venerable New York YC began to feel the strain. From 2,237 members in 1930, membership slipped to 1,515 by

A view of the stern of the Lightning shows the roomy cockpit and wide gunwales. Even with a crew of three, there is room for more.

Rosenfeld Collection,

Mystic, Connecticut

1937—a considerable loss in membership dues. The trend continued; in 1938 and 1939, 100 more sailors left the club than joined it, so in 1940 the club waived entrance fees for men under the age of 30, and reduced the annual dues of these new members to $75, down from $150 for regular members. To put that in perspective, $150 of those 1939-era dollars are equivalent to $1,860 in 2000.

While it might be stretching things a bit to call the 1930s the era of the dinghy, that might be a good term for a decade that saw the introduction of the Snipe, the Comet, and the Lightning dinghies.

The word itself comes from the days of Britain's long association with India. Members of the Royal Navy were fascinated by the utility of the small boats

With the Class B and the Interclub dinghies so similar in size and sail area, they raced together, as in this photograph. The differences in the two classes are subtle, except for the lapstrake hull of the Class B and the molded hull of the Interclub. *Rosenfeld Collection, Mystic, Connecticut*

used in Indian harbors to ferry passengers and light cargo out to seagoing vessels. These little boats, built locally and far handier than the heavy 14- to 30-foot double-ended tenders carried aboard their warships, were known by the Hindi word *dingi,* meaning, literally, "small boat." The word, with an Anglicized spelling, came to be applied to small, open boats generally, and the S&S Lightning, to many sailors, epitomizes the dinghy class. The Lightning, mentioned briefly in chapter 1, certainly deserves a closer look.

THE LIGHTNING

Olin Stephens drew the lines for S&S Design Number 265, the Lightning, in 1937, a project he characterized as "an intellectual, if not a financial, success." He sold the plans outright the next year, a move that influenced the business practice of S&S from that day forward. "As we watched the fleet grow we decided not to do that again," wrote Stephens.

The first officially recorded sail on a Lightning was with Rod Stephens at the helm, running the length of

New York's Lake Skaneateles in 1938. The genesis of the boat was a series of conversations between John Barnes, of the Skaneateles Boat Company, and several sailing friends in the Skaneateles area. These sailors wanted a boat big enough to daysail with half a dozen friends, but small enough to be handy to sail, and simple enough in design to be easily built at home. They also wanted it to be fast enough to race, with enough sail to make it exciting. To complete the usual wish list for dinghy design, they also wanted it to be inexpensive.

As noted, Stephens sold the plans outright. He had agreed at the outset of the Lightning project to sell the plans if a class organization were formed, and that happened quickly.

The Lightning had its public debut at the New York Motor Boat Show in January 1939. By the time of the show, nine builders had acquired a set of plans, with 20 boats already sold. Some of the owners met at the show, and the Lightning class organization was formed, practically on the spot.

The founders were explicit in the goals of the Lightning class. In the class constitution is a phrase that rings especially apt when considering it was written in the closing years of the depression:

> *To keep the Lightning class within the financial reach of a man of moderate means without handicapping ability or encouraging neglect in conditioning yachts . . . to rigidly maintain a strictly one design class, in order to positively insure that all Lightning class races held under the auspices of this Association be to determine the skill of the skipper and to eliminate all variations in the construction of the yachts.*

The Lightning, designed to be a family dayboat as well as a racer, was bigger than some of its dinghy kin, displacing 700 pounds and measuring 19 feet overall and 16 feet on the waterline. With that length, the beam—6 feet, 6 inches—didn't have to be excessive to make for a roomy boat. The 130-pound centerboard is deep, drawing nearly 5 feet when down, and the hard-chine design planes satisfyingly when pushed along by the 177 square feet of working sail. It's a spinnaker class, the additional 300 square feet of sail adding to the boat's downwind fun. It's no wonder the Lightning class is right behind the Snipe for sheer numbers of boats.

During the depression era, people devised all sorts of tests of character and stamina, perhaps to prove that their will and strength to survive ran a lot deeper than their pockets. With such sports as flagpole sitting and

marathon dancing becoming popular, it's no surprise that someone would stretch the proving grounds beyond the reaches of dry land.

FROSTBITING

In mid-July 1931, in the men's bar of the Larchmont Yacht Club, one of the sailors present challenged another to a race in dinghies on New Year's Day, 1932. Although the history of the event doesn't record what they were drinking, the stark times of the depression were as likely responsible as any particular type of drink. That the chilly practice of "frostbiting" began in the men's bar speaks volumes of the changes in yacht clubs since 1931, as well.

As word of the wager spread—New Year's Day was far enough in the future for word to spread quite far— other sailors thought the idea a good one, and wanted in on the regatta. The two wagerers evidently thought the more the merrier, and it turned into a proper regatta.

The race actually took place January 2, 1932, in the chill waters off the Knickerbocker Yacht Club in Man-

hasset Bay. The yachting editor of the *New York Herald Tribune*, William H. Taylor, took part in that first race, sailing his Ratsey International dinghy. James Robbins, yachting editor of the *New York Times*, was enlisted, and together they began to write about their exploits.

That first frostbiter dinghy, Taylor's Ratsey International, was a British design, known in England as a Lymington Scow, although its lapstrake-built hull shape was not what an American sailor would call a scow. When finally classified here in 1930, they became known as A boats. The A boats were lug-rigged with very sporty white-stitched red sails.

Winter dinghy racing soon became a regular event, aided in no small part by the coverage given it by both the *Times* and the *Herald Tribune*. Not to be outdone, other media began to cover the races, and the term "Frostbiters" showed up in print. Not long after that, the Frostbiters Yacht Club was founded, with a burgee showing a polar bear sitting on a cake of ice.

Some of the best sailors in the area began to show up at these winter contests, many of them in A boats. People such as Robert Bavier, Briggs Cunningham, Sherman Hoyt, Henry S. Morgan, Ernest Ratsey, and Cornelius Shields actively raced A boats in the frostbite regattas.

Shields took on the task of formulating rules and regulations for the A boats, which soon became the "official" boat for frostbiting, at least for a while.

Frostbiting soon took off—not surprising, given the widespread publicity, the mood of the times, and the level of competition afforded by the participants. The Larchmont Yacht Club was one of the first clubs to become active in frostbiting, and soon the limitations of the lug rig of the A boat engendered a desire for a better boat. John Alden, who sailed an A boat in Boston in that area's frostbite fleet, came up with his own design, but the clubs finally settled on the open B-class. Despite being an open class, the boats looked very much alike, and the design was introduced to the fleet in 1934.

The Naples Sabot is unique for the leeboard, mounted on the starboard side. It is very roomy despite being only 7 feet, 10 inches long, because there is no intrusive centerboard trunk.

Barbara Horner

(*previous page*) If you get your weight just right, you can nearly coax a plane out of the Interlake's strongly rockered hull. Although a hard-chine design, the bow is softened, making an easier entrance at slow speeds. Go a bit faster, and it lifts clear, reducing drag.

Jeff Thompson

The El Toro class of dinghy, designed after a lengthy "bull session" at San Francisco's Richmond YC in the Bay, has a shovel as the class' sail logo.

Kelly O'Neil

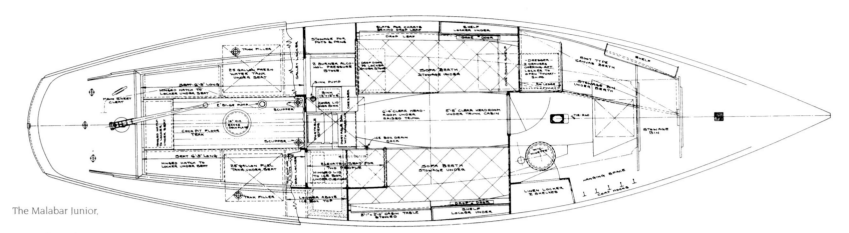

The Malabar Junior, especially in this version listed as Design Number 691, was one of Alden's most successful smaller auxiliary sailboats, with 27 of them built by the Bristol Yachtbuilding Company of Bristol, Maine. In 1939 they sold for $3,450 ($42,800 today) and the owner could specify a three- or four-berth layout. They came ready to sail, complete with kerosene cabin lights, cushions, life preservers, a whistle, bell, and fog horn, and two copies of the Pilot Rules.

John G. Alden Inc.

THE CLASS B BOATS

The person who "godfathered" the Class B was Cornelius Shields, who performed a similar role in the development of the International One-Design, designed by the Norwegian naval architect, Bjorne Aas, in 1935. Shields also championed the S&S-designed Shields class in 1962.

The B boats were built by several yards, including the Concordia Company, owned by Waldo Howland for 37 years. Howland's business partner in Concordia was Ray Hunt, who was well known as a superb sailor but whose true interest was in design. Howland financed the construction of a B boat to Hunt's lines, and a shipwright named Pat O'Connell, formerly of Lawley's yard, built the boat. That boat, *Plover*, was somewhat narrow but performed well at a frostbite regatta in Mystic, Connecticut, winning four of five races. *Plover* was sold at the end of the regatta, its winning record providing ample proof of the design.

Back at the drawing board, Hunt gave *Plover II* a bit more beam, and O'Connell again was contracted to build it. Howland and Hunt took the new boat to another frostbite regatta in Essex, Connecticut, a two-day

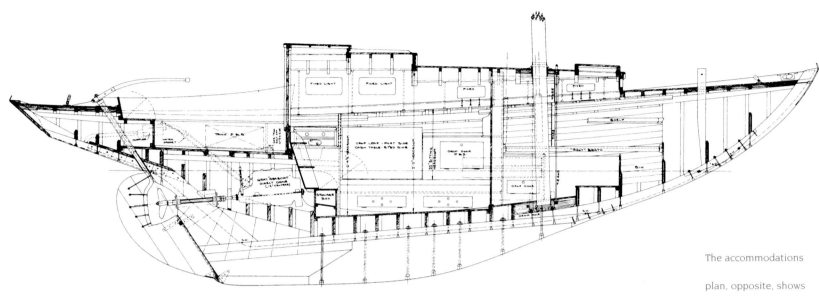

affair against a fleet of B boats. The boat was a success, dominating the fleet with a string of first-place finishes. The *Plovers*, initially built on spec, sold well, and it was a turning point for Concordia during the tough times of the depression. Howland and Hunt had wanted to make their company more than a brokerage firm. The *Plovers* gave the public proper notice that the Concordia Co. was in the design business.

Frostbiting at Larchmont grew in popularity, and was taken up by other Long Island Sound clubs. By 1939 these clubs expressed interest in having a boat designed specifically for frostbiting. Shields was instrumental in the development of the new frostbiting class, to be called the Interclub.

Answering the call, Sparkman & Stephens drew an 11-foot, 6-inch-overall dinghy based on a shorter, 9-foot, 6-inch dinghy already on their books. The new boat was an open cat-rigged dinghy made of molded mahogany veneer, was the same size as the Class B dinghies, and carried the same amount of sail—72 square feet. The Interclub was also identical in beam, at 4 feet, 7 inches, though there were minor rigging changes. It was a centerboard boat, weighing 200

pounds, and originally came with a jointed mast, allowing the rig to be disassembled and stowed within the boat, thus permitting their use as a tender when not racing and making cartopping or trailering easier.

The main changes in the design from the Class B were in the hull shape, done at the request of those racing the Class B boats. Because the Interclub was built from molded mahogany, the bow could be made a bit more bluff above the water, but with a sharp entrance. The frostbiters had been having problems with the Class B, which, with its fine entrance, could become unmanageable, even capsizing when running in a stiff breeze.

Construction of the new Interclubs began immediately. To ensure that the boats were built to the desires of the Larchmont sailors, Edward Waldvogel, a member of the club, supervised the process. Several builders, including the unlikely Zepher Furniture Company, constructed the first hundred boats of wood. In the 1970s, beginning at about hull number 200, the O'Day Corporation began to build them of fiberglass.

Some time later, when racing small sailboats in the winter had become an accepted practice, Taylor and Robbins were asked about their interest in promoting

The accommodations plan, opposite, shows sensible straight settees capable of doubling as sea berths and the forward head with the double-closing door. The high doghouse, while not everyone's favorite design feature, is decidedly practical. The overhangs, so graceful to look at, severely limit the interior space, despite clever and careful placement of the amenities. Note the tank locations, mentioned earlier in the text.

John G. Alden Inc.

frostbiting. Were they really that keen on sailing in the snow? Well, yes, they were, but after further questioning they also admitted there was more to it: frostbiting gave them something to write on yachting during the winter, which spared them from being assigned to cover basketball games.

In the center of the country, where frostbiting wasn't a sport (the water there froze solid, and "frostbiting" was done on iceboats), there was still an interest in the new classes of dinghies, despite the explosive growth in scows, as detailed in chapter 4.

In 1932, a group of sailors on the shores of Lake Erie, all members of the Sandusky Sailing Club, commissioned Francis Sweisguth to design a centerboard dinghy for the waters of Lake Erie and Sandusky Bay. The design requirements sound fairly familiar: it should be a good racing boat, with a crew of two or three, and capable of carrying four or more on a comfortable daysail. It had to be capable of being carried on a trailer, and be easy to sail. It also had to be affordable. There was one more requirement, this one solely with local conditions in mind: it had to be under 18 feet long, as that was the length at which the fees for dock use went from 25 cents a foot to 60 cents a foot.

The boat was briefly called the SC2, shorthand for Sandusky Sailing Club Class-Squared. But it wasn't called that for long. The Sandusky Sailing Club controlled the class at first, and in 1935 the club entered five SC2s in the I-LYA regatta at Put-In-Bay. By early 1936, however, a separate class association was formed and the name was changed to the Interlake Sailing Class, in recognition of its association with the I-LYA.

THE INTERLAKE

Sweisguth was a partner in the naval architecture firm of Ford, Payne and Sweisguth, based in Rochester, New York, and his fame in small-boat circles is ensured with the design of the Star. He set to work, coming up with the Interlake, an 18-foot centerboard boat, 15 feet,

3 inches overall with a beam of 6 feet, 3 inches. The boat displaced 650 pounds, and with the board down drew 4 feet, 7 inches.

The Interlake's rig, despite being designed in 1932, looks very modern, with a fractional headsail and a 125-square-foot, heavily roached main, made possible by the swept spreaders and no backstay. Working sail area totals 175 square feet, with a 110 percent jib. Despite the lack of a backstay the Interlake carries a spinnaker, a big one, measuring 200 square feet.

The waves on the shallow waters of Lake Erie and the bay typically are choppy and steep with a short period, and that certainly influenced the shape of the hull. The hard-chine hull, with considerable rocker, is somewhat similar to the Bug, but Sweisguth claimed the similarity was coincidental and in the eye of the beholder, not the designer. He had been asked similar questions before. In an interview in the Star class newsletter he was queried about the Bug being his inspiration for the Star. He replied, "I started from scratch, without looking at the Bug. If the two boats looked alike, it was because the lines of all chine-built boats with an arc bottom are similar."

The rocker and hard chine, coupled with the V-shaped bottom, truly did tame the local waters, and to Lake Erie sailors, who had been sailing on flat-bottomed dinghies, the change was noticeable.

The first Interlake was built at home by one of the members of the group that had conceived the project, who then took it to the Sandusky Boat Show. The Harry Darst Boat Company built hull number 2 for $90 ($1,160 in 2000 dollars), and three other members of the consortium also built Interlakes.

After the 1935 Put-In-Bay regatta, eight more boats were built, and the Sandusky SC became the home of Interlake Fleet Number 1.

The rocker certainly works to aid in the boat's maneuverablity, with turning leverage assisted by the transom-hung rudder. The simple rig has lent itself to

(*Opposite*) The 11-foot Moth class is for those sailors who want to race one-designs but who chafe under all those rules. Raced as a development class, nearly anything goes, within fairly broad limits. It is the biggest development class in the world, and provides its sailors the chance to design, build, and sail. Want to race a Moth? Build a hull no longer than 11 feet, beam no more than 5 feet, no lighter than 75 pounds. This Moth is distinctive for its flared bow and strong sheer.

Starke Jett

In the mid-1930s, Ernest H. "Cap'n Dick" Hartge, of the Hartge Yacht Yard in Galesville, Maryland, designed the Chesapeake 20, a 20-foot dinghy that was an "open" class, meaning it had to be within certain measurements, but anything not specified was "open," i.e., free of any restrictions. The resulting boat was fast, usually overcanvassed, and, in small numbers, continues to be raced today in the Chesapeake Bay. The Chesapeake 20 can provide a thrilling sail.

Starke Jett

The 1932 Olympics were held in Los Angeles, and this time the U. S. entered a team in three of the four classes: Star, 6-, and 8-meter. We didn't compete in the Monotype single-handed dinghy class. The U.S. Star team, skippered by Gilbert Gray with Andrew Libano Jr. as crew, took the gold medal with five firsts, a second, and a third. In the 8-meter class, U.S. skipper Owen Churchill also won a gold medal, while in the 6-meter class, Frederick Conant brought home the silver medal.

Elsewhere on the West Coast, 1934 was the year the San Diego Yacht Club clubhouse went for a cruise. Club members had been pressing for a change of location, and finally, after much debate, the clubhouse, measuring 60 by 70 feet, was placed on two barges borrowed from a lumber company and floated from Coronado to Roseville—a journey lasting just three hours. Set down on new pilings by the falling tide, it remained surrounded by water until harbor dredging deposited enough silt around the building that it once again stood on dry land.

the boat being used by sailing schools as the next step up from single-sail prams and dinghies.

Interlake sailors report their boats to be slightly slower than a Thistle, but more capable in choppy seas and faster to tack.

On the West Coast, 1932 brought some good news, at least for sailors. Sailing had been an Olympic event since the first games in 1896—an academic distinction, since the sailing events that year were all cancelled due to the weather. In 1900, the U.S. Olympic sailing team entered the competition, but didn't bring home any medals. Apparently stung, it wasn't until 1928 that a U.S. sailing team again competed, with the same results as 1900.

── EL TORO AND SABOT DINGHIES ──

There are two little favorites of sailors that made their appearance in the 1930s—the El Toro and the Naples Sabot dinghies. The El Toro was first conceived at the Richmond Yacht Club, a San Francisco Bay sailing club that had its start in 1932 with a dozen sailors who met in a tin shed belonging to a club whose idea of going out on the water required outboard motors.

The Richmond YC, which was proud to call itself the "Poor Man's Yacht Club," began with a Snipe fleet. Around 1936, "bull sessions" at the club kept coming back to the need for a dinghy even cheaper and smaller than the Snipe; when *Rudder* published plans for the MacGregor Sabot design in 1939, the club adapted it to their own uses. To recognize the El Toro's beginnings, the Richmond YC chose a shovel as the class emblem: what would be handier after a lengthy "bull session" than a shovel?

The El Toro is truly diminutive, measuring an inch less than 8 feet, allowing home builders to use a single standard sheet of plywood. It is only 3 feet, 10 inches on the beam, with a single cat-rigged sail of 49 square feet. Despite all that, it is loved in measure beyond its size, especially in the San Francisco Bay area. The 80-pound displacement and relatively larger centerboard make for good sailing manners, and racing is quite competitive. Although dinghies of the El Toro's size are usually thought of as youth trainers, adults sail them with a seriousness out of all proportion to the diminutive side of the dinghy, and they are very popular as tenders on larger boats.

At the end of the decade, the country had begun to feel the chill winds of war. In Europe, the fighting had begun, and coastal security regulations severely limited yacht racing. Boats could not be out after dark, and identification numbers, extending from the gunwale to the waterline, were painted on the bows.

Sailboats were commandeered by the Navy for coastal patrols, and clubs began to see a drop in membership as sailors volunteered for military service. It was not a good way to end a decade, but the 1930s were a decade that many people were glad to see come to a close. ✳

The wooden Moths are perhaps the prettiest of the fleet. Note the split tiller handle. While there are Australian, British, and International Moths, unreconciled rule differences between the various "species" prevent them from competing against one another.

Starke Jett

chapter eight

Dawn of the Fiberglass Era

Sailboats of the 1950s

*E*very year, the New York Motor Boat Show, held in Grand Central Palace, was the venue to introduce the new crop of sailboats, despite the "motor" part of the name. In 1950, there was a brave new world of sailboats at the show, characterized by one word: *fiberglass.*

By the 1950s, the design of pleasure boats had become a discipline of its own, and the inspiration from working boats, in most cases, was visible only to eyes capable of discerning slight traces of genetic material. Cargo capacity was not a factor; the cargo of these boats was people, and sailors expected more comfort and protection from the elements than had ever been possible in a working boat. With the thinner hulls possible due to fiberglass, boats had more room below, and the idea that small boats could safely carry a family on an extended cruise or even offshore was no longer seen as the ravings of someone who had spent too much time at sea. The real revolution, of course, was as much in the mindset of the sailing public as it was in the materials.

In 1959, the Henry R. Hinckley Co. introduced the Bermuda 40, a Bill Tripp design, at the New York Boat Show.

Traditionalists were appalled, but there were more people who were impressed. The seagoing centerboarder combined

a shoal draft of just over 4 feet with 33 percent ballast ratio, a heavy displacement-to-length ratio of 394, and a very

cruiser-oriented sail area-to-displacement ratio of 16.43 to make a boat that was comfortable, seaworthy, and, when

the wind blew, won races. *Onne van der Wal*

The 1950 New York Motor Boat Show was a watershed event all because of a material virtually unknown to the sailing public at the time: fiberglass. Although you see only wooden boats in this photograph, lurking just out of sight is Carl Beetle and his Beetle Swan. *Mystic Seaport, Rosenfeld Collection, Mystic, Connecticut*

In the 1949 show, there were seven boats made of the new material. The average new-boat purchaser still had basically one choice in construction material and that was wood: wooden boats, built on production lines with stacks of precut ribs and planking awaiting installation on the series of hulls in what amounted to a production line. There were metal boats, of course, and ferrocement, but the latter, despite having proven itself in the "Mulberry" floating docks used in the D-Day landing, was an orphan then as now, used almost entirely for one-offs or home-building projects.

In 1950, despite the misgivings expressed by some of the yachting journalists who reviewed the show, the end of wood for production boats was on the horizon. Molded plywood was seen by many of the postwar writers as the future for boatbuilding, despite the problems with plywood only being flexible in one plane. Hard-chine designs and faux-clinker designs, using strips of plywood, marched off the designers' tables, but fiberglass allowed the graceful sweeps of sheer and compound curves that wood had afforded, with all the savings of production in quantity.

The cost, from the consumer's viewpoint, was the beginning of a certain design homogeneity: to amortize the cost of making the molds, engaging the services of a naval architect, setting up a factory, and hiring and training a work force, many boats had to be built. If consumers were uncomfortable with this, their discomfort was not evident in sales numbers.

Initially, fiberglass boats were no cheaper than wooden boats. In a 1950 article in *Yachting* magazine, William H. Taylor, discussing the New York Boat Show, noted that none of the boats in the show were over 20 feet long, "but bigger plastic hulls have been built. For the present, however, plastics enthusiasts expect the process to

Fiberglass as a material to build boats wasn't totally new. In the 1947 show, with the smoke barely cleared from the battlefields of World War II, Carl Beetle showed up with his 12-foot cat-rigged Beetle Swan, by some accounts the first fiberglass boat to appear at the prestigious New York show.

THE FIBERGLASS REVOLUTION

Ray Greene's Rebel was also introduced in 1947 and was initially cat-rigged, but soon evolved into a fractional sloop. The credit for the first fiberglass sailboat is thus a tie for first place, with both Beetle and Greene starting the revolution the same year.

The response of the buying public at the 1947 show was restrained, to put it politely. There were no sales; not until Beetle removed the fiberglass seats, coaming, and deck did he sell his boats. But this consumer skepticism was short-lived.

be used principally in smaller craft, due, for one thing to the high cost of tooling up for molding big boats."

Some people figured molded plywood would be the way of the future. At the 1950 show there was a 26-foot racing sloop made of molded plywood. The material had been proven in wartime construction of seaplane floats, among other things, and of course plywood lent itself well and easily to home construction, although the heated molds for plywood were confined strictly to industrial use.

There were other materials competing with fiberglass. In the postwar boom, manufacturers had built boats using various plastics developed during wartime, but most of the new materials were unsuitable for one reason or another: the plastic required heat to set; it had inconsistent strength; voids introduced by the molding process required hours of hand labor to fill and fair, and so on. The list of problems with other plastics was a long one, giving fiberglass the winning edge.

Yachting magazine described consumer resistance to fiberglass, and how that was changing, in its reports on the 1950 show. Taylor wrote,

In the past, there have been various kinds of plastic used in boatbuilding; various substances and fabrics used to hold the resin together and give it the requisite strength and other qualities. This year every plastic hull in the New York show had a Fiberglass base, though each firm is keeping its own methods and the ingredients other than Fiberglass that go into the hull, under its own hat. There is some resistance, with manufacturers carrying the torch for plastic boats butting their heads persistently and expensively into the traditional conservatism of yachtsmen. . . . They made converts, and like converts to all faiths, some of them became fanatics.

Either you like them or you wouldn't have one in your front yard to plant flowers in.
Now, the builders report, the feeling has changed. It may be partly because old-line builders like Anchorage and Cape Cod have gone into building in plastic the same boats they build in wood, that the material is readily accepted by the public.

The Beetle Swan is of sufficient historical importance that one of them has been donated to the Museum of Yachting in Newport, Rhode Island. This is one of the early models, which was cat-rigged. The later Swans came as a sloop. The deck is simply dropped over the molded hull, with an overlapping edge, like the lid on a shoebox. *Matte Gineo*

(*page* 146)
The Hinckley 36 is an example of that company's best production years for traditional construction— the 1950s. *Alison Langley*

The manufacturers themselves were observing a sea change. At the 1947 show, Beetle left with as many boats as he'd arrived with; by 1950, according to one manufacturer, "we used to have to sell a customer plastics and if he was sold on the material he'd buy our boat. Now we have to sell our boats in competition with other people's boats. The mere fact that a boat is plastic doesn't build up a wall of sales resistance as it used to."

Certainly, the new material wasn't yet selling on the basis of cost. Prices at the 1950 show were comparable for fiberglass and wooden boats. It was not yet clear whether advances in production technology would bring down costs for fiberglass.

Manufacturers were convinced that fiberglass was the future for their industry, and they invested time and research into improving the material and production techniques. The boats they produced proved long-lasting and eliminated most of the annual chores associated with wooden boats, freeing their owners to spend more time on the water.

REVOLUTIONARY SAILCLOTH

About the time that fiberglass was accepted, Dacron became available as a sailcloth. While cotton continued to be used for a decade or so, Dacron quickly dominated the market, and, in a pleasant change from the usual, this technological revolution benefited those sailors with less money more than it did the wealthy.

In the days of Egyptian cotton sails, racers who could afford it had a collection of sails to match the wind, from a light sail for those afternoon zephyrs to a boardlike heavy-weather sail. The larger the inventory, the more nearly one could match sails precisely to the wind, but a Dacron sail, strong even in the lighter weights, would work over a much wider range of winds, and the need for sets of sails to match each number of the Beaufort scale vanished. A sailor could do well with one or two sails, reducing at least in one way the gap between wealthy sailors and those of more modest means.

With the increased strength of Dacron, designers discovered that rigging needed to be beefed up. Previously, the cotton of the sail was often the first thing to go: seams would rip out, boltropes would pull loose; cotton weakened by water and mildew would just come apart. Now, shackles were snapping, sheets parting, and shrouds breaking.

The answer was stainless-steel shackles, stronger wire for standing rigging, Dacron line, aluminum spars and masts, and stronger, geared winches. Aluminum had been used in masts for some time, and its price came down as more and more manufacturers took advantage of its combination of strength, light weight, and resistance to corrosion.

Boats didn't go appreciably faster—technology hadn't done anything about the laws of physics—but they could go faster longer. Winds that would have damaged cotton sails just put a good strain on a Dacron trysail.

The Bounty II sloop, a joint effort of Philip Rhodes and William Garden, was an early effort at making a fiberglass boat from a design that had its origins in a wooden boat. The first large stock auxiliary sailboat produced in fiberglass is *Oreole* II, hull number 15. *Mystic Seaport, Rosenfeld collection, Mystic, Connecticut*

As manufacturers expanded their use of fiberglass, and improved construction techniques, they reduced their costs to the sailing public's benefit. Between 1950 and 1960 the average wage in the United States grew by some 30 percent. Labor-intensive items such as wooden boats were getting very expensive, and although fiberglass didn't build itself, the skills it required could be taught more quickly. Once a mold was made, a fiberglass boat could be turned around more quickly and with less labor than its wood counterpart.

Ray Greene's Rebel is still being built and raced, and even though the design is now more than 50 years old, it has aged well. In light airs, the boat still moves easily, with its broad, flat hull offering little resistance. *Jeff Thomas*

The methods used in early fiberglass boats varied as the technology developed. Early boats used matching metal or wood molds. The fiberglass was laid over a male mold, and then, a female mold was set down over it and pressure was applied, along with heat. The method worked, but it was expensive and slow. For one thing, it required two molds. The development of polyester resin made construction simpler because it allowed the use of either female or male molds, and the resin would set at room temperature.

Soon, builders realized that the mold itself could be made of fiberglass, thus completing the circle, technologically, eliminating the use of wood or metal entirely in the building process.

Once the building methods were worked out, it was full speed ahead for the fiberglass boat industry. Some of the builders of wooden boats were quicker to catch on than others. In an interview in the January 1950 issue of *Rudder*, E. L. Goodwin, president of the Cape Cod Shipbuilding Co., noted that although Cape Cod would continue the building of wooden boats "such as the Cape Cod Baby Knockabout, Interlake Rhodes 18, the Mercury and the Minx, any future development [would] be in fiberglass."

─────────── THE BULLSEYE ───────────

Cape Cod had already begun building the Herreshoff Bullseye (to which it had exclusive rights) in fiberglass by 1950. Initially, fiberglass was used primarily to make smaller boats, as it was a new material, and builders weren't entirely certain about its strength (or even its longevity).

At the 1955 New York Boat Show, this one held at the Armory, a 15-foot fiberglass boat was raised 15 feet in the air and dropped onto the concrete floor, at the urging of television producers looking for good footage. The boat bounced, to the relief of the builder. There is no record of the response of the TV producers, who may have been hoping for something more dramatic than a demonstration of fiberglass' strength.

Bay-area skipper Tom Newton's Triton, *Captain Hooke*, hull number 259, makes its way across San Francisco Bay in a glorious breeze with its spinnaker flying. The Triton changed the way people thought about "plastic boats." They were seaworthy, tough, and priced right. It didn't hurt that they looked good as well. The first circumnav in a fiberglass boat was made in a Triton. *Courtesy Tom Newton*

Carl Beetle is on record for shooting a .38-caliber revolver at a fiberglass boat to demonstrate its strength, and a West Coast fiberglass boatbuilding company called Yacht Constructors employed what amounted to a small arsenal to conduct its tests. Using, in turn, a .22 long, a .38, a .45, and a .30/06 rifle, they shot a sample of fiberglass full of holes and satisfied themselves as to its strength.

In the late 1950s, designer Bill Tripp, perhaps lacking a closet full of firearms, drove his Jaguar XK-140 over fiberglass panels lying in his driveway as a strength test: he was designing the Vitesse 40, which eventually became known as the Block Island 40.

While the above materials-testing regimens seem a bit crude by today's standards, they are a good index of the seat-of-the-pants designing and building philosophy of those early days. Once designers proved the material with the use of firepower, cranes, and sports cars, it was time to introduce larger fiberglass boats.

The first auxiliary sailboat to be built of fiberglass was truly a milestone in terms of both designer and consumer acceptance. Philip Rhodes created it for Coleman Boat Works. Although it was produced in the 1950s, it derived, as did Coleman's decision to hire him, from a wooden boat Rhodes made for the company in 1939 (the same

year he made the 11-foot, cat-rigged Penguin dinghy). With considerable help from William Garden, Rhodes drew a 38-foot sloop designed for four people. He called it the *Bounty*. The idea was to use assembly-line manufacture to build an easily handled family cruiser that would be affordable to a nation still shaking off the effects of the Great Depression. The boat was introduced at the 1940 New York Motor Boat Show, complete with a 25-horsepower inboard, and sold for $3,875, equivalent to $47,500 in 2000 dollars. It was an amazing success, with the Coleman Boat Works selling one boat a week—as fast as they came off the production line. The success was a short-lived one, however, because the war in Europe would soon consume the nation's attention and resources. The original *Bounty*'s production ended just as it was getting started.

After the war, the Coleman Boat Works continued building wooden boats (following a move from their earlier East Coast headquarters to Sausalito, California), but success on the scale of the prewar *Bounty* eluded them. Working with the same design philosophy (i.e., a small, affordable family cruiser), Coleman again hired Rhodes, who brought Garden in on the project. This time, Coleman wanted a fiberglass design, convinced, as were other manufacturers, that fiberglass was the future of recreational boating. Both designers had drawn fiberglass boats before, but neither of them had any experience in what the scantlings should be for a fiberglass boat that would measure nearly 41 feet overall.

The new boat was to be called the *Bounty II*, yet its similarity to the prewar *Bounty* was largely conceptual. The lineage of *Bounty II* is more accurately traced to a 1955 Rhodes design called *Altair*. Bodie Rhodes, Philip's son, scaled down *Altair*'s lines, but only slightly. The wa-

terline, for example, went from 29 feet to 28. The boat was slender, by today's standards, with a beam of 10 feet, 3 inches on the overall length of 40 feet, 10 inches, and was relatively deep of draft at 5 feet, 10 inches.

The real work was in designing for fiberglass, which involved far more than merely scaling-down an existing

The 20-foot Highlander dinghy class was designed in 1951 by Gordon Douglass. *Jeff Thompson*

design intended for a wooden boat. When there was any doubt, Garden, who drew the scantlings and the deck mold, played it safe by making the hull and the deck thicker.

The *Bounty II* was the star of the 1957 New York Motor Boat Show. Coleman sold four boats at the show. The price was $18,500, the equivalent of $113, 380 in 2000 dollars, a good value for a boat measuring over 40 feet overall and ready to sail away. The *Bounty II's* popularity grew, and in the period after the show, 16 boats were sold, with another dozen built by the Palmer Johnson yard in Sturgeon Bay, Wisconsin.

Production of bigger boats brought a renewed interest in testing fiberglass. In 1952, Coleman Boat Works, which had become, briefly, Coleman Plastics, was renamed Aero-Marine when two new business partners joined the firm. Vincent Lazzara, one of the partners (and the inventor of the snap-shackle, according to an article in *Nautical Quarterly*), revived many of the established structural tests, kicking the hull, dropping it from a 50-foot crane into the water, and shooting it with .38-caliber bullets to prove its strength. They even took people sailing— which probably opened more wallets than the other tests combined.

Fiberglass was truly coming into its own with the *Bounty II;* another first was the fiberglass mast, made of unidirectional fiberglass and weighing half what a comparable aluminum mast would weigh. The first boats were overcanvassed, however, and proved to be too tender, so the original 7/8 fractional rig was changed to a masthead rig with a shorter, aluminum mast for greater stability. Buyers could choose from a sloop rig, with 714 square feet of sail area, or a yawl rig, with 799 square feet.

The *Bounty II* survived all the tests, and over a hundred of the Rhodes boats were sold. In the 1960s, the boat was still being made (see chapter 9). *The Bounty II* was used for competition and for cruising, and showed up in such races as the Transpac, the various Bermuda races, and the Detroit–Macinac Race, where the design proved both itself and the practicality of fiberglass.

The Triton was perhaps one of the most significant of the boats of the 1950s (although it truly hit its stride in the 1960s). Designed by Carl Alberg to a request for

The Herreshoff 12-1/2, now made by the Cape Cod Shipbuilding Co. in fiberglass and called the Cape Cod Bullseye, has the added luxury of a small cuddy. *Mary Jane Hayes*

a 28-foot sailboat that would sleep four, he succeeded admirably. The boat debuted at the 1959 New York Motor Boat Show and was an immediate success. Seventeen boats were sold during the show, and in the years to follow, 712 of them were built. The Triton measured 28 feet, 4 inches overall, on a waterline of 20 feet, 6 inches. The short waterline relative to overall length was a function of the then-popular CCA rule, which resulted in long overhangs. As the theory went, it allowed an increase in waterline as the boat heeled, thus providing "free" (i.e., unrated) length.

The boat developed a deserved reputation for seaworthiness. With a ballast ratio of 38 percent, displacing 8,000 pounds and coupled with the full keel, the boat has initial tenderness but stiffens after about 15 degrees and then tracks well. Skinny, in the manner of all of

One of the unforeseen benefits of fiberglass construction has been the spread of local classes to areas far from their origin. You can test sail a new type of boat, a far more certain means of determining if you like it, rather than look at plans and then build it. The El Toro dinghy, discussed in chapter 5, was almost entirely a West Coast boat until it began to be built in fiberglass. Now, there is even a fleet in the nation's capitol. *Walter Cooper*

Alberg's boats, Tritons have a beam-to-length ratio of 3.43. That was indicative of how far yacht design had come by that time, and the Triton was considered to be a beamy boat.

Much of the boat's initial success was due to its attractive price. In 1959, a bare-boat Triton sold for $9,700 ($57,000 today), a price that was roughly a third of the price of a custom wooden boat at the time.

The Triton came in two variants, an East Coast version, with a fractional rig, and a West Coast version, with a shorter mast and a masthead rig, designed for the gusty winds of San Francisco Bay. There were also a very few built as yawls. The West Coast version was built by AeroMarine in Sausalito, California, and was somewhat heavier as well. The AeroMarine Plastics factory built between 125 and 200 Tritons; numbers vary depending on the source, but all agree the West Coast boat was heavier, and some owners will maintain they were better built as well.

The East Coast boats, built at the Pearson yard in Rhode Island, had other differences besides the mast height. East Coast Tritons had wood coamings and trim, which were all plastic on the West Coast boats.

Another popular boat, which made the transition to fiberglass gradually, was Ray Greene's Rebel. Although introduced in 1947 and first sold in 1948, the Rebel came into its own in the 1950s. The first Rebel regatta was held in 1950, and an owners' group, at first called the Association of Rebel Sailors, was soon founded by one of Ray Greene's early dealers, Lud Fromme. By 1952, the association had grown to a national organization, called the National Rebel Class Association (NRCA).

The Rebel, 16 feet, 1 inch long and initially cat-rigged, was designed jointly by Greene and Alvin Youngquist, whose "day job" was teaching drafting at a local high school. Greene wanted to make a daysailer that was inexpensive to buy and easy to sail, without making any compromises in the "fun factor." Greene also wanted

the boat to be relatively heavy, as he thought the boat would be a good match for Great Lakes conditions, where gusts would knock over a lighter boat.

Perhaps taking a cue from Beetle, who found buyers reluctant to buy a boat made entirely of fiberglass, Greene made the Rebel with wood decks until 1955, when the Rebel finally became an entirely fiberglass boat.

The Rebel weighed 700 pounds, not bad for a beamy centerboard sloop (they were only cat-rigged for the first year or two), with a beam-to-length ratio of roughly 2.4 that was designed to have a bit of heft. The year Greene introduced the boat, he sold 25 of them, and by the time of the 1950 boat show, sales had doubled. The reception at the boat show solidified its success, and the Rebel was soon being sailed on both coasts and many of the small lakes in between.

Bill Lapworth, designer of the Cal 20, grew up in Detroit, where he raced on local catboats, of the type mentioned in chapter 4. He was the in-house designer for Jensen Marine, and the Cal 20, designed at the end of the 1950s, was the company's hot rod, with a 46 percent ballast ratio and a light displacement-to-length ratio of 149. *Mariah's Eyes*

Greene was as good at marketing as he was at designing. For a number of years after the formation of the NRCA, Greene included the first year's dues for the association with the purchase of every new Rebel. Later, with the introduction of the Mark I standard Rebel, the boat popped out of the mold some 15 pounds lighter than class specifications, allowing owners to ballast the boat as needed or add racing gear.

Price, the most vital part of any small boat design, was something Greene watched with a critical eye. His thinking was that a dinghy under $1,000 would sell a lot more quickly than one even a dollar over that magic number, and so the line was drawn—$1,000, not a penny more.

In 1952, a Rebel could be purchased, sails and all, for $948 ($6,000 today); the only available option, nylon sails, was an additional $120. The boat's low price, and Greene's determination to keep it low, explains why Greene, working from his factory in Toledo, Ohio, was able to sell an average of one Rebel every three days for 25 years until the business was finally sold in 1973.

The Rebel used thermo-setting fiberglass, baked at 300 degrees Fahrenheit for two hours on a wooden mold. The resin was from Owens-Corning Fiberglass. In 1949, a U.S. government–initiated antitrust lawsuit forced Owens-Corning to share fiberglass technology with, among other companies, Libby-Owens-Ford, which helped foster one of the Rebel class' most treasured trophies, the Libby-Owens-Ford Perpetual Trophy, passed along each year to the class champion. It was first awarded in 1955, and it might not have been merely coincidence that that was the year the Rebel finally went to all-fiberglass construction.

All sailors cherish in their heart memories of the boat they learned to sail on: it's right up there with first love. For many sailors, especially those on the East Coast, that boat was the 13-foot, 6-inch Blue Jay. Designed by Sparkman & Stephens as a junior sailor, with all the rigging of a "real" boat, the Blue Jay carried a main, jib, and a voluminous spinnaker, which when set more than doubled the sail area of the main and jib together.

While designed in 1948, the Blue Jay came into its own in the 1950s. That was the year the design was adopted at both the Manhasset Bay and the Larchmont yacht clubs, and it was an immediate success. Hard-chined, it was easily built, and with its S&S heritage, it was thought of as something of a "kid sister" to another well-loved S&S boat, the Lightning.

The Blue Jay was not a trendsetter in materials the way the Swan and the Rebel were. It was built of plywood, a material fairly new at the time, and one thought by some to be the boatbuilding material of the future. But making boats of plywood still required a boatbuilder's touch, and that caused plywood to inevitably lose out to fiberglass on the factory floor.

Although made of plywood, Blue Jays were light: class rules minimize all-up weight at 275 pounds. With a protective coaming on the forward portion of the cockpit, no seats—thus requiring the sailors to stay low in the boat—and class rules that required an anchor to be carried, as well as bailing equipment and a paddle, the boats were, if nothing else, safe. One more class requirement was nearly radical, especially considering the time: lifejackets were required to be carried on board when racing.

The idea was to have a boat for junior sailors that would fly a spinnaker, with a short, fractional sloop rig. Blue Jays were thought of as a transition boat from the Optis or other simple boats to more complex, larger keelboats. The boom and the foot of the jib were both drawn fairly high, in the interests of safety for those young sailors not fully aware of the dangers of a jibing boom, and the high-cut jib allowed good visibility when racing.

Even though it was targeted at young sailors, the Blue Jay also appealed to adults, who may have encountered them first with their children. The boats were designed to be user-friendly, a term that didn't exist in 1950 but would have if there had been more designs at the time for which no other term was so perfectly descriptive.

Within a year, there were big fleets of them. At the Larchmont YC, during the 1954 Race Week activities, a fleet of 38 Blue Jays showed up, and by the end of the 1950s, fleets of several hundred were on the starting line at national regattas.

The Blue Jay's stability was legendary, especially for a centerboard boat that drew only 3 feet, 9 inches. During the 1954 Race Week mentioned above, a brief, intense squall roared across a fleet of Blue Jays and Lightnings. Only one Blue Jay capsized, while there were many Lightning crews in the water, perhaps wishing they had chosen a more stable boat.

The decade of the 1950s was a time of great foment in the sailing world. Between the wonders of fiberglass and a relatively healthy economy, more and more middle-class families were taking to the water. Boats were being designed with the needs of a family in mind, a family that was no wealthier than any of the others

who were moving into another 1950s phenomenon—the suburbs.

Sailing was no longer the bailiwick of the wealthy or the eccentric loner heading off for parts and horizons unknown. Magazines, advertising, and designers all had begun to realize the existence of a new market: ordinary people. The stage was set for "ordinary boats," and about then, the 1950s turned into the 1960s. ✳

chapter nine

Grand Fiberglass Classics

Sailboats of the 1960s

By the 1960s, sailboats had entered the era of fiberglass. The miracle plastic, no longer seen as such a miracle—and hopefully with its gunshot- and crane-drop testing days behind— fiberglass began to appear everywhere. There were fiberglass dinghies, daysailers, coastal cruisers, and offshore boats. The Tom Gilmer–designed Allied Seawind 30 *Apogee*, skippered solo by Alan Eddy, became the first fiberglass boat to circumnavigate the globe, in the years 1963–1969. Eddy would have been second to young Robin Graham, who began a circumnav aboard a Lapworth 24 in 1965, but Graham's journey was interrupted. He completed the voyage in a Luders 33, five years later. Both voyages confirmed the worth of fiberglass boats to a sailing world that was pretty much convinced by then anyway, judging from the numbers of such boats being sold.

In Eddy's case, an encounter with whales and a grounding on a reef near Fiji failed to damage the boat, and despite the boat's size, measuring only 24 feet on the waterline, he made good time, averaging better than 160 miles noon-to-noon from the Galapagos to the Marquesas,

The 585 *Tartan* 27, introduced in 1961, S&S Design Number 1617, was the company's first fiberglass design. Named for the overall length, it is 21 feet, 6 inches on the waterline, has a relatively narrow 8-foot, 7-inch beam, and draws 3 feet, 2 inches with the centerboard up and 6 feet, 4 inches with it down. The 27 displaced 7,400 pounds with a ballast ratio of 33 percent. It is the most popular of all American production cruisers. *Billy Black*

On the occasion of the Sunfish's 50th anniversary in November of 2000, 104 of the 13-foot dinghies gathered in the waters of Sarasota Bay, Florida. Although designed in 1951, the Sunfish familiar to everyone was designed in 1960, made longer, wider, and of fiberglass rather than the original wood. *Doran Cushing*

with a best run of 179 miles. He wrote a book, more of a promotional piece about his experience and the Allied Seawind boat, called *So You Want to Sail Around the World*, which was, not surprisingly, published by the Allied Boat Company.

The 1960s brought a decade of boats that we still see on the water, sailed and loved by their owners. The sheer numbers of popular sailing craft from this decade force could fill one or more volumes on their own. Some of the more famous of the 1960s-era boats are the Cal 40, introduced in 1963; the Bermuda 40 (actually introduced in 1959, but first sold in quantity beginning in 1960); most of George O'Day's beloved small boats; the Gary Mull–designed Santana 22, built by the W. D. Schock Company in Santa Ana, California; the Tartan 27, designed by Bill Shaw; and, of course, the wonderful, wee, and well-loved Sunfish, which began to be built in fiberglass in 1960.

The Sunfish, 2 inches short of 14 feet overall, is simplicity on the water. One mast, one sail, one string to pull, and in 1960 it sold for $195, complete. To put that in perspective, that is $1,130 in 2000 dollars.

The progenitor of the lateen-rigged Sunfish was the Sailfish, designed in the years just after the end of World

War II by Alex Bryan and Cortland "Bud" Heyniger and made of mahogany, with all the shortcomings of that material. They had formed a company named Alcort, after the first syllable of each of their names, to build boat kits for returning GIs who wanted to get out on the water inexpensively. The Sailfish was little more than a board with a sail, but when Bryan's wife discovered there was no place to put her feet when she became pregnant, according to a brief account in Daniel Spurr's *Heart of Glass*, the two men expanded the design, putting in a diminutive "cockpit" and creating the Sunfish—a boat which, by itself, probably introduced more people to sailing than any other single boat design.

Between 1959 and 1960, the Sunfish was redesigned for fiberglass construction. It became longer, by 2-1/2 inches, and an inch wider, and the wood mast was discontinued, replaced by an aluminum one. Now, Alcort had a boat that was cheap, durable, and easy to sail, the Holy Grail of all small-boat designers. With that, the Sunfish took the world of sailing by storm. You didn't need to be a sailor; you didn't even need to know how to sail. The boat was virtually self-explanatory. To go sailing, you only needed to tie it to the roof of your car and find some water. Setting it up took a few minutes, and with the deeper hull and broader beam of the new fiberglass Sunfish, it was stable enough that beginners could make their way across a lake the day they bought one.

Hot on the heels of the successful Triton came the Tartan 27, designed in 1960 by Bill Shaw of the Sparkman & Stephens studio. The 27, a centerboarder with a full keel, was offered by Tartan Marine, of Grand River, Ohio, as a sloop or a yawl, but most of the purchasers went for the single-stick version. At 27 feet overall, it was 18 inches shorter than the Triton, but the waterline length was nearly a foot longer, giving it, on paper at least, a hull speed that was incrementally faster by just 0.1 knot, but the charms and attraction of the boat went far beyond calculations. Beamier, by just 4 inches, there was more room below, and with its masthead rig, compared to the fractional rig of the Triton, the 27 carried slightly more sail and displaced fully half a ton less than the Triton. The yawl rig carried nearly 400 square feet of sail, with the sloop sporting 375 square feet.

The 27 was finished somewhat better than the Triton, and it sold well, with more than 700 of them built. The design was crafted to work well under CCA and Midget Ocean Racing Club rules. One of its early racing victories was at the Larchmont Yacht Club Edlu Trophy Race in 1962, when a Tartan 27 took the trophy in a field of 86 boats, winning on corrected time but beating many larger boats on actual time as well. As with any boat that meets with commercial success, the price was right. In 1963, you could sail away on a Tartan 27 for $11,750, equivalent to $66,100 in 2000 dollars, and with the Triton listing for $11,500 at the same time, the Tartan looked very good to sailboat buyers. It was the first boat offered by Tartan Marine, and an auspicious start for this company, which sells yachts to the present day.

By the middle of the decade, something like 2,000 sailboats were being sold every month, a number that was unimaginable a dozen years previous. With the growth of sales, an equivalent growth in design took place. Bigger, faster, and more affordable boats were coming off the ways, and boats came to the market that weren't like anything seen before.

William Lapworth is the man who drew the boat that changed forever what people thought of as a production offshore racer. His design was the Cal 40, built by Jensen Marine in Costa Mesa, California. Remember when boats looked like their work-boat antecedents? That was then. The Cal 40 was very much now, circa 1963, and the first ones to hit the water went on to win nearly every ocean race they entered. That included the 1965 Southern Ocean Racing Conference; the Transpac in 1965, 1966, and 1967; and the 1966 Bermuda Race. In 1966, Ted Turner took home all the marbles in the SORC with his Cal 40 *Vamp X*.

The Cal 40 started with a clean slate, and was designed for the water, for speed, and for production in fiberglass. Despite a spade rudder that was considered at

The Pearson Invicta, designed in 1960 by Bill Tripp, was a 37-foot centerboard yawl. In 1964, an Invicta was the first fiberglass boat to win the Bermuda Race, and it has become a trusted boat for many cruisers. Tom Zydler

The Alberg 30, Carl Alberg's next big success after the Triton, was made for 25 years. Measuring 21 feet, 8 inches on the waterline, and with a beam of 8 feet, 9 inches the displacement sloop had a decent ballast ratio of 36 percent. *Onne van der Wal*

the time to be dangerously exposed behind the long fin keel, this was a boat that looked fairly familiar above the water. It had a boxy cabin, even a tiller, which seemed almost out of place on a boat that measured nearly 40 feet overall, but Lapworth knew what he was doing. To see what made this boat the harbinger of things to come, you only had to look beneath the water.

The numbers tell much of the story. With a hull speed of 7.37 knots and light displacement-to-length ratio of 250, the Cal 40 is at the light end of what is thought of as a "medium" boat.

The Cal 40's spade rudder was placed well aft, nearly at the waterline under the overhung stern, and with a relatively modest sail area of 699 square feet pushing 15,500 pounds through the water (producing a sail area-to-displacement ratio of 18.06, more cruiser than racer, but in the "cruiser-racer" category) its well-balanced rig made it easy to steer.

The hull shape was as unique for the times as the spade rudder-fin keel, with a flattened forefoot and flatter bilges that, like a dinghy, allowed this big boat to surf when things went right.

Fiberglass construction made this shape possible. A wooden boat with such large, nearly flat areas would require large framing timbers of such size that weight would become the limiting factor. Instead of surfing on the water, a wooden version would probably pound its way through it, giving up much in speed, maneuverability, and sailing enjoyment.

Separating the keel and the rudder, although thought to be virtually as revolutionary as the hull shape, was not original with the Cal 40. In 1892 Nathanael Herreshoff put a spade rudder aft of a fin keel on *Wenonah* (which had an underbody remarkably similar to the Cal 40), and it worked well enough for racing purposes that rating rules made it uncompetitive. The practice was abandoned for cruising boats and the larger racing boats until more than half a century later.

The Cal 40, measuring 39 feet, 4 inches overall with a waterline of 30 feet, 4 inches, was 11 feet on the beam, and drew 5 feet, 7 inches. These were measurements—especially the beam-to-length ratio— that got it into trouble when the International Offshore Rule (IOR) came into effect, especially coupled with its relatively light displacement. In a design review in the March 1980 issue of *Sailing* magazine, Bob Perry said he thought that "the IOR killed the Cal 40's production run" at an early age, roughly 170 boats.

The Hinckley Co., long known as a maker of exquisitely built wooden yachts, had resisted, at least publicly, the shift to fiberglass. But in 1959, Henry Hinckley decided to build a fiberglass boat, from a mold to be taken from a 38-foot wooden yawl called the *Sou'wester Sr.* Before that could happen, the Hinckley yard was asked by a group of eight sailors, who had been in touch with Bill Tripp, to modify the Block Island 40 to their specifications, and they wanted Hinckley to make the boat in fiberglass. Hinckley made the boat, called it the Bermuda 40, and while some diehard wooden boat fans took verbal umbrage, the first boat was a success. It was delivered to one of the group of eight, and, although unfinished at the time, placed well in the 1959 Bermuda Race. Later, a Bermuda 40 won the Northern Ocean Racing Conference trophy in 1964 and the Marblehead to Halifax race in 1965.

The Bermuda 40, full-keel with a centerboard, displaced 19,000 pounds, with a relatively low ballast ratio of 29 percent. With the cast-bronze centerboard down, the Bermuda 40 drew 8 feet, 7 inches, and this long lever arm certainly contributed to stability. Yawl-rigged with 725 square feet of sail (later versions offered a sloop rig),

(*top left*) The Cal 40 *Victoria* cuts a fine figure on its native waters of San Francisco Bay. Bill Lapworth based the design on his L- series of wood racing boats, but completely redrew the scantlings and modified the lines in a manner that could only be done with fiberglass. *Mariah's Eye*

(*bottom left*) The 1963 Islander Bahama, designed by J. H. McGlasson, was the first design to come from Islander Yachts of Costa Mesa, California, which started business as Wayfarer Yachts, in Irvine. Many of Islander's boats of that time featured flush decks. Waterline length is 20 feet, with a beam of 7 feet, 10 inches. The Bahama displaced 4,200 pounds and carried 1,700 pounds of ballast, driven by 280 square feet of sail. *Mariah's Eyes*

the numbers for sail area-to-displacement work out to 16.35, on the low side of what is thought of as a cruiser, while the critical calculation of displacement to length is 395 for the first version (going up to 416 for the Mark III), which, even in 1960, made it a heavy boat.

Although the boat was raced, and often, it really was a cruiser. Beamy for its day, owners could load it up for cruising, as it settled only an inch into the water with

the addition of 1,800 pounds of cruising gear. The Bermuda 40's sea manners, in part because of the heavy displacement, were impeccable. The full keel, drawing 4 feet, 1 inch with the board up, was ever so slightly cut away at the forefoot, but on the whole, the underbody was not revolutionary. The Bermuda 40 was well made, dependable, sailed well, and attracted a following that bordered on fanaticism. The boat went through three major design evolutions, each time gaining a bit of sail area, mast height, and, just to make sure it didn't turn into a racer, displacement.

Testimonials to the boat's strength, comfort, and generally good design abound, and when hull number 203 hit the water, it was the end of the longest production run—1959 to 1991—in the world of fiberglass auxiliary sailboats.

Carl Alberg had another winner in 1962, designing for Pearson Yachts (bought by Grumman Allied Industries in 1960), when he penned the Ensign. A nifty little daysailer with a full keel, the Ensign was 16 feet, 9 inches overall, displacing 3,000 pounds with 1,200 pounds of lead ballast, giving it a ballast ratio of 40 percent.

The Ensign began as the Electra Daysailer, which was a redesign of a boat Alberg had done under another Pearson commission, this one to design a 22-foot cruiser that could compete in the Midget Ocean Racing Conference. The Electra 22, introduced in 1960, sold well. The factory was turning them out at the same rate as the Triton, three a week. Over a six-year production run, some 350 Electra 22s were built, complete with a galley, head, and berths for sailors who could get by with minimal space. The boat was seaworthy; the masthead rig gave it a lot of sail, and the cockpit, although cozy, was self-bailing.

The boat was small, too small for comfortable cruising, and many owners found themselves spending more time in the cockpit and less in the cabin (*saloon* is almost too much of a word for the diminutive space belowdecks in the Electra 22). Prospective customers said they saw the boat more as a daysailer than a mini cruiser, so Pearson went to Alberg and asked for another design touchup. This time he wanted the cockpit larger and the cabin smaller, transforming the boat into a one-design daysailer.

Alberg thought well of the idea. In a letter to the Ensign class association newsletter in 1975, he said he thought "the idea was quite feasible since the Electra's displacement was quite light and the daysailer's would be even lighter."

There was more to it than merely enlarging and shrinking. The mast was moved forward 6 inches, the mainsail was made bigger, and the masthead rig of the Electra 22 was changed to a fractional rig. The cabin became more of a cuddy, and the cockpit became luxurious, half the length of the boat. Alberg was right about the weight savings: the redesigned Electra 22 shed 2,000 pounds, while maintaining the half-ton of inside ballast, fitted into a molded cavity in the one-piece hull. The hull was unchanged.

A comparison of the numbers is revealing. The Electra carried 227 square feet of sail, and the Ensign 201. Plugging in those numbers gives a sail area-to-displacement ratio for the Electra 22 of 17.51, and 15.5 for the Ensign, making a real shift in power from the heavy end of the cruising range to off the heavy end of the cruising range. Even more telling is the displacement-to-length ratio. Although the ballast ratio changed from 33 to 40 percent, displacement-to-length was unmatched at 285.

Pearson continued to build the hull as though it were a MORC racer, using 1.5-ounce mat and 24-ounce roving in both layers.

The new boat was called the Electra Daysailer initially. In 1962, when the first one hit the water, 219 of them marched out the door of the Pearson yard in the old Herreshoff works in Bristol, Rhode Island. With the number of Electra Daysailers being sailed, an owner's association wasn't far behind, and shortly after the boat's

introduction a number of their owners met to discuss forming an association. One of the first items to come up, one not at all on the agenda, was that everyone hated the name Electra Daysailer, feeling that it did not sufficiently distinguish the boat from the original, very different, Electra 22. They came up with the name Ensign, the factory agreed, and now, with upward of 1,780 Ensigns built, the Ensign is the largest class of one-design full-keel sailboats in the United States.

George O'Day deserves mention as a man whose company specialized in small boats. The boat that really put his company on the map was a 16-foot Day Sailer. Uffa Fox, an Englishman, designed the Day Sailer, along with many other O'Day boats. The company sold 13,000 Day Sailers. His company had its start with the Rhodes 19, designed by Philip Rhodes. The 19-foot

The Pearson Electra Daysailer, designed by Carl Alberg, was a heavily built mini-cruiser, despite the Daysailer moniker. The cabin was minimal, but the boat could stand up to anything a sailor would be likely to face if he had the sense to remember that it was just a 22-foot-long boat. *Rosenfeld collection, Mystic, Connecticut*

(*opposite*) The *Bermuda* 40 *Cygnus* enjoys some good sailing in the waters on Massachusetts Bay. The B40 went through three variations, each adding sail area and displacement. The Mark III, 1,000 pounds heavier than the first model (called the "Custom"), was a foot longer on the waterline from being down on its marks. *Mary Jane Hayes*

Many sailors think the Pearson Ensign was what the Electra should have been all along: a sturdy, heavily ballasted true daysailer, without losing cockpit space to a cabin that was more a hideout than it was living space. This Ensign earns its keep as part of the Milwaukee Community Sailing Center fleet. *Greg Jones*

(*opposite*) The Columbia 40, first built in 1964, was developed by Columbia Yacht Corp. from Charley Morgan's Sabre, which narrowly missed winning the 1964 SORC championship. Possibly the 40's most unique feature is the steel skeleton that reinforces the hull and spreads the load of the shrouds. A total of 55 C40s were built between 1964 and 1969. *Starke Jett*

Ericson Yachts, of Irvine, California, produced a series of 20- and 30-foot yachts, many of them Bruce King designs, like this Ericson 35. Fast, with a fin keel drawing an inch less than 5 feet, the hull was tank tested to refine the form. Waterline length is 25 feet, 10 inches, beam is 10 feet, 10 inches, and displacement is 11,600 pounds, with 5,000 pounds of lead ballast. Sail area is 533 square feet. This Ericson, heading out the Golden Gate, is fitted out for cruising, a fine retirement plan for a 1969 racing boat. *Mariah's Eyes*

sloop was offered as either a centerboarder or a keelboat, and over 2,200 of them were sold.

The Mariner was basically a Rhodes 19 underwater, but instead of the open cuddy of the Rhodes, the Mariner had a small cabin. There were 3,338 of them sold during a production run from 1963 to 1972. The Mariner came in a keel or a centerboard version, displacing 1,435 and 1,305 pounds, respectively.

O'Day kept his sights firmly fixed on his customer, the small-boat sailor who wanted a simple, easy-to-sail boat, capable of being trailered to his favorite lake and sailed with a minimum of fuss. An early O'Day brochure states that "all O'Day boats are easily sailed by the novice sailor," and he meant it. It wasn't until 1971 that the first boat over 20 feet was marketed under the O'Day name. For the 1960s, George O'Day was the man who put small boats within the reach of anyone with the desire.

The Bristol 35, designed by John Alden and introduced in 1966, was built to the CCA rule, with all the design hallmarks of that rule. Alden never made a boat that didn't delight the eye, and the 35's graceful sheer, coupled with nearly 11 feet of overhang, produced a boat that looked as good as it sailed. The full keel was coupled with a centerboard, giving it the combination of shoal draft and windward ability for offshore work that made the boat a winner.

Clint Pearson, brother to Everett Pearson of Pearson Yachts, started Bristol Yachts. The Pearson 35 was part of a lineup that featured some of the best designers in the country, from Alden to Alberg to Tripp to Halsey Herreshoff. Pearson's tactic of enlisting prominent designers, rather than having a single "house designer," worked very well, with Pearson able to market a range of boats in

which each boat had its own character, determined by the designer rather than the factory.

The Bristol 35 was one of Bristol Yachts' stars. The copywriters for the company's brochures, fully aware of what racing meant for customer attraction, and equally aware that most owners spent more time on board with their families than they did racing, advertised the boat as "a racing yacht with fine accommodations."

Measuring 34 feet, 8 inches overall, the overhangs, while lovely to look at, made for a waterline only 23 feet, 9 inches. There were two versions offered, a sloop and a yawl, three if you count the deep-draft version, drawing 5 feet, as opposed to the centerboarder's 3 feet, 9 inches. The 35 carried 5,200 pounds of ballast, encapsulated in a keel cavity, with a displacement of 12,500 pounds, pushed by 531 square feet of sail. That works out to a ballast ratio of nearly 42 percent, and a (very) heavy displacement-to-length ratio of 414. They could be thought

of as slightly underpowered with a sail area-to-displacement ratio of 15.83, but Bristol never marketed the 35 as a racer. If there was any doubt as to the design purpose of the boat, buyers need look no further than the standard water tank: 130 gallons. With the tank full, that would add another half-ton to the boat's displacement.

While the boat was certainly built to a price (as are virtually all production boats) with a sailaway price of $18,000 in 1966, it was priced to sell. Bristol Yacht's customers didn't show up with blue blazers and white yachting caps; they were ordinary people who wanted to go sailing, and Bristol was there to help them enjoy the water, at an affordable price.

Built to sell didn't mean they scrimped on material. Conventional wisdom at the yacht club bar has it that early fiberglass boats were overbuilt "because they didn't know how strong the stuff was," and to a certain extent that's true. But they also didn't know how to reduce the resin to a minimum. It is, after all, the fiberglass that gives the

Bill Crealock worked at Columbia Yacht Corp. during the late 1960s and early 1970s, when the company had factories on both coasts and was cranking out a dizzying variety of boats by some of the country's best designer. The Columbia 28 dates from the late 1960s, although it continued to be made as the 28 Mk II in the 1970s. *Mariah's Eyes*

material its strength; resin just holds it together. Hulls on the 35 near the turn of the bilge could be as much as an inch thick, and even if more of it was resin than would be a modern builder's preference, it still produced a strong hull. Hulls were solid fiberglass, mostly woven roving, with the cabin and deck cored with plywood.

The hull shape was fairly conventional. From the spoon bow, a cutaway forefoot ran back to a full keel, with a rudder tucked under the overhanging stern. Overhangs were both the good news and the bad news on the Bristol 35. Lovely to look at, and providing a welcome increase in waterline when heeled, the price paid was reduced room below deck. The accommodations weren't helped by the narrow beam, either. A beam-to-length ratio of 3.48 helped the 35 slip through the water nicely, but kept things cozy in the saloon.

The cockpit had lovely, long seats, and a companionway offset to starboard: not the best thing for that ultimate wave, but well suited for the interior layout. The Bristol 35 was very much a boat of the times, and built sturdily enough that they still show up at marinas, anchorages, and sailboat brokers.

When Bill Schock moved his boatbuilding company to Santa Ana, California, he began a new line of boats, the first of which was designed by Gary Mull. Exactly 22 feet overall, he called it the Santana 22, and in 1965 it must have been the right boat. Over 700 of them were finally sold, and somehow Mull shoehorned four berths into the little cruiser.

The story among Santana 22 sailors has it that Mull and Schock were talking about the Cal 20, designed by Bill Lapworth in 1961 and built by Jensen Marine. The Cal 20, 20 feet long and displacing 1,950 pounds, was enjoying some success and Schock wondered what might be done to improve on the boat.

After realizing that what Schock was really saying was "design a boat better than the Cal 20," Mull set to work and the result was a little cruiser with a deck-stepped mast (the Cal 20 had a hinged mast) that was 2 feet longer and displaced 2,600 pounds.

The two boats have some similarities, but Mull really did draw a different boat. The Santana 22 is 22 feet overall, and 18 feet, 8 inches on the waterline. Beamy, at 7 feet, 10 inches, there was as much interior room as you could put on a little boat that still has aspirations of going fast.

The masthead sloop rig of the 22 (the Cal 20 was fractionally rigged) carried 217 square feet and the boat displaced 2,600 pounds, with the 1,230 pounds of iron ballast, giving the Mull design a credibly stiff ballast ratio of 47 percent.

A light displacement-to-length ratio of 176 and the cruiserlike sail area-to-displacement ratio of 18.41 made the boat just right for the winds of San Francisco Bay, home waters of the W. D. Schock Corp. With lots of stability, a sail area that wouldn't overpower things, a light displacement that made it easy to handle, a fast fin keel, slanted aft with a spade rudder, the boat immediately became popular, and an active class association was soon founded, setting up fleet number 1 in the Bay Area almost as soon as the boat was introduced. The boat was accepted as a one-design class in both the Yacht Racing Association (YRA) and the Small Yacht Racing Association (SYRA). The YRA allowed spinnakers, but the SYRA restricted the boat to its original main and the 130 percent overlapping jib.

The boat's popularity grew, and fleets were active all along the West Coast, soon spreading to the East Coast and the Midwest.

Despite its intention as a coastal and protected-water sailor, the boat is sturdy; a few Santana 22s have made the trip west from California to Hawaii during delivery from the factory. They suit their owners well, and the racers seem to prefer the boat in its main-and-jib racing trim. The class association dropped out of official participation in the YRA over the issue of the spinnaker; even though there has been some talk of joining again, racers and cruisers who either enjoy or desire Spartan accommodations

take out their little 22s and sail them like the little big boat they are.

The decade of the 1960s was a vibrant time for American sailboats, and any book on the boats of that era that covered them all would probably sink all but the biggest. Times were good for the boat industry, fiberglass was cheap, and it was accepted as a boatbuilding material. Wooden boats became rarities, loved by their owners but even they knew, deep in their hearts, that they were loving what amounted to a dinosaur.

It looked like this would go on forever. New companies were being formed all the time, making boats in garages, small factories on the edge of town, and in established yards that had made the switch to fiberglass, sometimes reluctantly, sometimes with the enthusiasm of the newly converted. Boats were being turned out by the thousands, but it wouldn't last forever. Things would soon change, and the era of the 1970s and its volatile politics would play a bigger role than anything the boat-buying public or the factories could imagine. ✳

(*opposite*) The Santana 22 was designed to beat the Cal 20, but it wasn't a boat-for-boat match. With the Santana being bigger and heavier, it was more boat. *Mariah's Eyes*

The Cal 20, selling for roughly $500 less than the Santana 22 and weighing 450 pounds less (which made it easier to trailer), continued to be popular with sailors, but it is interesting to look at the two boats to compare Gary Mull's Santana to Bill Lapworth's Cal. *Mariah's Eyes*

The Age of Innovation

Sailboats of the 1970s

*T*he growth in American boating had been little short of spectacular in the years leading up to the 1970s. In 1970, 51,000 domestically produced sailboats were sold, with that number nearly tripling by 1972 at 114,000 boats. The curve continued to climb—120,000 in 1973 and 143,000 in 1974—but by 1975, politics had entered the marine world.

In the Middle East, prices for crude oil had remained practically constant from 1948 to 1957, when adjusted for inflation. From 1958 to 1970, the price of crude oil actually dropped. In 1960, the Organization of Petroleum Exporting Countries (OPEC) was formed, with Iran, Iraq, Kuwait, Saudi Arabia, and Venezuela as the first five members, but the price of crude oil continued to drop. By 1971, the oil-exporting countries faced a serious drop in the value of their only product. Adjusted for purchasing power, the price of a barrel of crude had dropped by 40 percent, and OPEC's membership increased as Algeria, Indonesia, Libya, Nigeria, Qatar, and the United Arab Emirates joined the cartel.

Then the war started. In 1972, a barrel of crude was about $3. On October 5, 1973, Syria and Egypt attacked Israel. That day, Yom Kippur on the Jewish religious calendar, gave its name to the war. The United States and many other countries in the west backed Israel, supplying

Tartan Yachts really hits its stride by the 1970s. The 37 was a modified version of a Ted Hood design, done for Tartan, called the Black Watch. The 37 was made of solid, uncored fiberglass. It was a deep-water boat, drawing 9 feet, 4 inches, and relatively narrow, with an 8-foot beam. The T37 carried 618 square feet of sail. *Mariah's Eyes*

everything from moral support to arms. In response, the Arab members of OPEC imposed an oil embargo on those countries and by the end of 1974 the price of a barrel of crude had jumped to $12. Nearly all of that 400 percent price increase occurred in less than six months.

The point of this short detour into politics is that fiberglass resins are a petrochemical, and their prices are directly linked to the price of oil. The answer was better design, a more careful analysis of the stresses involved, and a consequent lessening in the thickness of the material. When that reduction in thickness was preceded by careful stress analysis, the result was a lighter boat that sailed better. When it was established empirically, sometimes the scantlings were too thin. For the most part, though, the inherent strength of fiberglass allowed the change in construction, and the 1970s era

was a time of innovation and the construction of better boats, built to be affordable.

It was also a decade of big companies. The 1960s had seen many yards coming and going, others were absorbed by larger companies, and the 1970s were no different. Boatbuilding is a chancy business. A few unsold boats in the yard, for a small company, can represent a big part of their capital, so turnover is crucial. A temporary slowing of sales can be a death knell for an otherwise healthy business.

In 1973, John and Warren Luhrs decided to start a sailboat manufacturing company. It wasn't a new idea for them; the Luhrs family boatbuilding tradition went back to the 1800s, three generations removed, with Henry Luhrs, a German immigrant. The Luhrs had stayed involved with boats ever since, until 1965, when they sold their business to Bangor Punta, a timber conglomerate. To keep their hands in the boat business, John and Warren bought Silverton Sea Skiffs of New Jersey. They changed the name to Henry Luhrs Sea Skiffs, and then, in 1973, they formed Hunter Marine.

The first Hunter sailboat was a 25-foot sloop, designed by John Cherubini, who went on to design a long list of some of Hunter's best boats, including the 25, 27, 30, 33, 36, and 37 Cutter and the hull of the 54. The 25 was an immediate success. Designed in the first part of 1972, the boat went into production in 1973. Although it was conceived as a family cruiser (with racing input from Bob Seidelman), it really was a successful boat on the race course. In a brief review of the boat in *Sail* magazine's annual sailboat directory in 1974, the writer stated that as of the end of July, the 25 had "never lost a formal race in competition throughout the country."

John Cherubini Jr. wrote on the Hunter owners' Web site that the design of the Hunter 25 "was very clearly a collaborative effort," with the senior Cherubini providing "the design and technical know-how," and Seidelman providing his knowledge regarding racing

In 1974 the Hunter 30 was introduced, a cruising centerboard boat with a hand-laid hull, good sailing manners and a price hard to resist. A 1975 Hunter 30 sold for $19,995.

Starke Jett

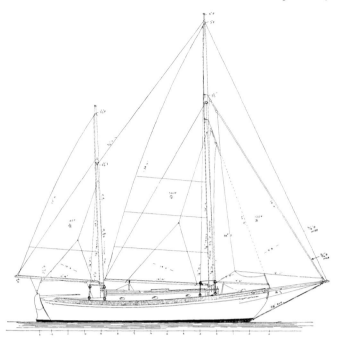

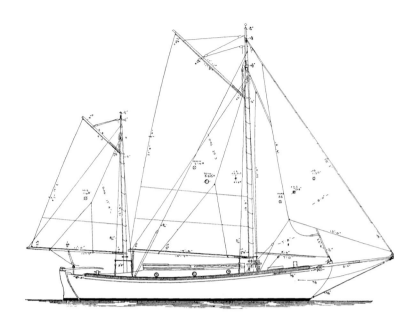

requirements and what the market might want in a small racer-cruiser. The racing part was pretty successful, as the H-25's sail area-to-displacement ratio rated as 19.2 with the IOR's 1967–1968 revised rules; the marketing goal was to get it to 18 "which few 25-footers ever did," noted Cherubini Jr. He added that they did not want the boat to rate as a quarter-tonner. The Midget Ocean Racing Conference rating was 18.0–18.2.

The Hunter 25 was most certainly a child of the 1970s. The fin keel, although very squared-off in outline, was absolutely contemporary. Two versions were offered, varying only in draft. The deep-draft keel (the Hunter marketers managed to refrain from calling it an "offshore keel") drew 3 feet, 11 inches, and the shoal draft drew a foot less. The boat sailed well, with a sail area-to-displacement ratio of 18.29, barely into the cruiser-racer category, and speed was helped with a light displacement-to-length ratio of 210. But what probably endeared it most to sailors graduating to their first keelboat was the high ballast ratio of nearly 47 percent, enough to keep the boat on its feet and the crew out of the water.

The next boat down the ways at Hunter was the Hunter 30, truly a step up, in both size and design. Sole

credit for this design lies with John Cherubini, and his hand is evident everywhere you look.

The elongated fin keel, drawing 4 feet, has a centerboard that pivots down, increasing draft to 5 feet, 3 inches, and a rudder hung from a full-length skeg. Thanks to a beamier hull shape, the 30 has more usable room below. The length overall, measuring the barest half-inch under 30 feet, is carried on a 10-foot, 1-1/2-inch beam, with 25 feet, 9 inches on the waterline. As with the 25, the ballast ratio is high, 44 percent using Hunter's 1975 published displacement of 9,500 pounds. In a correspondence on the Hunter owners' Web site, John Cherubini Jr. noted that the 30's true displacement was 10,002 pounds. Using that figure, the ballast ratio is still high, at 42 percent, so the 30 was a boat that could stand up to a breeze.

Hunter's success is due in part to its delivering a lot of sailboat for the money, and even in the early days the company instinctively knew that sailboats sell from the inside out. Thus, the Hunter 30 had a cabintrunk that might seem a bit large, and carried too far forward, if viewed with eyes focused only on aesthetics. The payoff, though, was in the saloon, where you couldn't see that nearly a

Atkin's original drawings show Eric rigged as a ketch, with either a gaff or a bermudan rig. The gaff set 588 square feet of sail and the bermudan 726. Atkin said he would choose the gaff "if I were going off on deep water," while admitting the bermudan would be faster. It was John Alden who suggested the change to a cutter. Note the club-footed jib, just as used on the Westsail 32.

Courtesy William Atkin

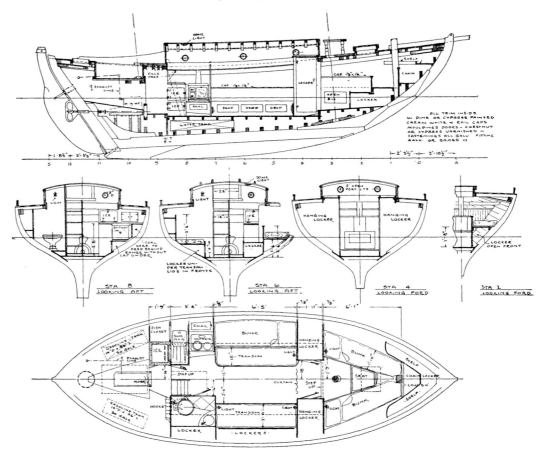

The deck plan of the 32-foot LOA Eric shows a classic double-ender, nearly identical fore and aft, with a small cockpit and nearly all living space confined to within the center third of the boat. The sectional drawings clearly show the deep, wine-glass hull, a concession to seaworthiness over performance. In profile, the hull shows the Archer influence; indeed, Atkin calls Eric "a Colin Archer ketch." The Atkin touch was evident in the raised coachroof, necessary if a 32-foot boat, even one with such a deep hull, was to have standing headroom.

Courtesy of William Atkin

third of the boat's above-water profile was in the cabin-trunk. It was a 30-footer with 6 feet, 3 inches of head-room all the way forward to the V-berth. Contemporary reviews speak of the boat as having accommodations that "make it seem like a 35-footer."

With all that comfort, it was still a fast boat, and, for the times, a light one, with a displacement-to-length ratio of 221 and a sail area-to-displacement ratio of 15.89 (using the "official" displacement). The saloon included a feature that was fast disappearing on pro-duction cruisers—the pilot berth, set to port above the settee, and a quarter berth, also to port, giving two sea berths when on a starboard tack but just one on the port tack.

The 1970s era was a time of social change. People would tell you with a perfectly straight face they were "finding themselves," having previously, one assumes,

lost themselves. Magazines ran articles about people do-ing heretofore unheard-of things with their lives, from living in teepees to following bands around the coun-try. Politics, the Vietnam War, student unrest, and "the Pill" made for a decade that only vaguely resembled the previous one.

The perfect boat for the 1970s generation was, it seems, the Westsail 32, which began modern life in the middle of the 1960s. The boat had a checkered past, and early literature is inconsistent as to who designed it. A 1975 sailing magazine credits Colin Archer with the de-sign, but another source lists the designer as "Colin Archer, William Atkin et al." In fact, it was W. I. B "Bill" Crealock who transformed the Archer–Atkin design into the Westsail 32.

The creation of the Westsail 32 is an interesting story, worthy of a fairly complete telling. It starts in

1872, almost exactly a century before the first boat to bear the name was built.

Archer drew his first pilot boat in 1872, designing the flush-deck double-enders for seaworthiness rather than speed. Most of them were cutter-rigged, with the mast farther aft than had been the practice. A few were ketch-rigged, but as the pilot boats were typically sailed with a minimal crew, the cutter was an easier rig to sail short-handed.

In 1887, shortly after this double-ended craft became the accepted boat for pilots, the fledgling Norwegian Society for the Rescue of the Shipwrecked (abbreviated in Norwegian NSSR) approached Archer to design its first rescue boat. With the launch of the 45-foot *Colin Archer* in 1893, the NSSR became operational.

The *Colin Archer*, 45 feet on deck, carried 15 feet, 3 inches of beam and displaced a very sturdy 27 tons. It was fully decked over, double-planked, with four watertight bulkheads—this was a boat that would keep sailing in any weather to effect a rescue at sea. The *Colin Archer* had a loose-footed gaff main, a large staysail, and a loose-footed gaff mizzen.

In one of the first NSSR rescues, the *Colin Archer* rescued 22 people in a violent storm and brought them to harbor. Soon, Archer's boats had a worldwide reputation for seaworthiness. Archer never thought of himself as a designer of racing boats, or even yachts, although Archer's double-enders were used as both.

In 1924 Archer's designs came to the United States via William Nutting, whom we met in chapter 1 as the editor of *Motorboat* magazine. Nutting went to Norway, saw the Archer boats, and was particularly taken with a 47-foot rescue boat. He and his cruising buddy, Arthur Hildebrand, put their money together and figured they could afford a 32-foot version of the 47-foot lifeboat. Nutting took photographs of the plans and made a skeleton hull model of the smaller version. Nutting and Hildebrand liked the model, but thought it would sail better if the bows were slightly finer.

Upon their return to the United States they talked with William Atkin and had a set of lines drawn, but with the sections farther apart from amidships forward. This "stretched" the forward part of the boat, which in the Archer version was practically a mirror image of the aft section.

They showed the result to John Alden, who agreed with their hull modification, as well as their plan to rig it as a cutter rather than using Archer's ketch rig. This modified Archer-Atkin design became a gaff cutter, which was to measure 32 feet overall, 27 feet, 6 inches on the waterline, with an 11-foot beam and drawing 5 feet. It was to displace 19,000 pounds with a sail area of 790 square feet.

The design was called Eric, but when Nutting learned he could have it built more cheaply in Norway, he decided not to proceed with construction, and instead published the plans in *Motorboat*. There was so much interest that Atkin drew a slightly modified version, with the same dimensions but with an even finer bow and slightly less displacement. This change shifted the center of buoyancy aft of amidships. He cut away

Eric with a flush deck is almost exactly a scaled-down Colin Archer, the 45-foot rescue boat. This more nearly resembles the Kendall 32, the "first" Westsail 32. Only minor changes are evident in the layout, most notable being the 50-gallon water tank in the bow of the flush-deck version, with the chain locker aft and below the tank. *Courtesy of William Atkin*

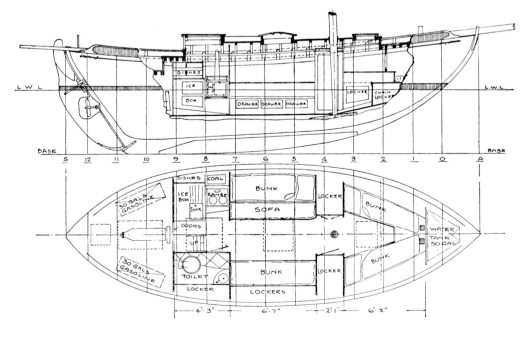

Westsail the world! That was the slogan used in Westsail's pacesetting advertising campaign, selling, not the boat, but the adventure that came with it. It worked, and the world of cruising sailboats was changed from that moment forward. Westsail owners thought of themselves as heading for that far horizon.

Michaelle Wetteland

The Morgan 24 had a centerboard, with the rudder separated from the keel/centerboard assembly; not a new idea, but one which endeared the boat to racers for its ability to turn quickly and, with the board up, reduce wetted area. This pair of 24s get ready for rounding the downwind mark. *Doran Cushing*

the forefoot and increased the sheer, making it prettier and better balanced. Three boats were built, at first named *Faith, Hope,* and *Charity,* but the owners changed the names to *Freya, Valgeda,* and *Eric.* They were rigged as ketch cutters, allowing a larger cabin as a result of the mast now being a foot forward when compared to the cutter version. The new Eric set 588 square feet of sail.

The Westsail 32 arose when a group of would-be cruisers led by a carpenter named Larry Kendall in Costa Mesa, California, commissioned Crealock to take the lines of the Atkin-designed Thistle (a later version of the Eric) and turn it into a fiberglass boat. When Crealock sat down to design the boat, he had much to work with. It was a proven design insofar as seaworthiness was concerned, vastly overbuilt of wood and refined through the efforts of two truly great designers.

Kendall, meanwhile, bought an ad in *Yachting* magazine telling people about the boat, which he called the Kendall 32. It was a tiny ad, only an eighth of a page, the smallest ad he could buy that wasn't in the classified section. Over 5,000 people responded and Kendall decided

to become a boatbuilder. By the end of the 1960s he had yet to deliver a boat, and the molds for the Kendall 32 were auctioned at a bankruptcy sale.

A couple named Snider and Lynne Vick attended the auction. Snider was an engineer and Lynne had a background in consumer marketing and advertising. It would be fair to say they were novice sailors, but they couldn't resist the lure of a chance to become boatbuilders. They got into the business for just $1,800, which purchased the molds for the Kendall 32, and paid a month's rent in advance on a place to build boats.

It was a package deal: they also bought the addresses of the 5,000 would-be Kendall 32 owners and they kept running the ad. There were three people whose boat construction had been stopped in mid-build when Kendall went bankrupt; the Vicks wrote new contracts with them and went back to Crealock for a design tweak, putting a cabin on the flush-decked Kendall 32. By 1971, the first Westsail 32 was built, just in time for the 1970s.

A look at the Westsail's measurements reveals that Crealock didn't stray too far from Atkin's Eric. Here are

the numbers: 32 feet overall; 27 feet, 6 inches on the waterline; 11-foot beam; and 5-foot draft. The Westsail had 500 pounds more displacement than Eric, but with less sail—629 square feet, down from 790 square feet. Ballast was 7,000 pounds. Flying the 120 percent gennie put up 483 square feet of sail; main and genoa together add up to 786 square feet. So how do the numbers stack up? The displacement-to-length ratio is a very heavy 419; the sail area-to-displacement ratio of 14.7 with working sails is off most charts (with main and 120 percent gennie it goes up to 17.4—in the middle of the cruiser category); and the ballast ratio is a stable 39 percent. Heavy, slow, stable, the 32 appealed to people with a romantic image of sailing off to the South Seas, not sailors racing around the cans on Wednesday night. The Westsail 32 was escape, dreams, salt-spiced freedom. It

was also one of the most overbuilt fiberglass boats ever produced. Two layers of gelcoat were applied over 12 alternating layers of mat and roving. The deck was reinforced with half-inch marine plywood, and 2 inches of plywood were under the deck-stepped mast.

All this was bannered under the general heading of "safety." The Westsail 32 would get you home, albeit slowly, from anything you might meet out there as you "found yourself." That was how the boat was sold.

Marketing is all about selling sizzle, not steak, and the Vicks started putting out a newsletter called *Windbag,* sending it to everyone who responded to the ad. They learned that the builders of sailboats had been ignoring those people, whether sailors or wannabes, who saw sailing as a way to slip the surly bonds of shore. These people weren't interested in racing, and had no desire to sail a Spartan boat designed for speed, or even one built for luxury.

They wanted the sizzle, and Westsail wanted to sell it to them. The Westsail dealers didn't have showrooms; they were either "cruising stations" or "cruising centers." At the cruising stations, the sales staff, selected because they were sailors, seemed to prefer talking about the South Seas, white beaches, and palm trees rather than such boring things as performance numbers.

Then the *Time* magazine editor showed up. He wanted to write a story about cruising sailboats and the people who were sailing them; it was one of those defining moments in the history of the Westsail Corporation. The article came out, four pages of the glories of getting away from it all by the simple expedient of buying a boat that—even to a complete lubber, maybe especially to a complete lubber—looked exactly like a sailboat should: bowsprit, swoopy sheerline, bronze fittings, wood trim, and all those palm trees somewhere just over the horizon.

The orders flocked in, faster than the factory could fulfill them, probably faster than two factories could, even if another had existed. The Vicks literally couldn't make Westsails fast enough, but to keep the ball rolling they took the money, guaranteed a delivery price, and kept building. Then the price of oil took off like a big bird, followed closely by the price of fiberglass. Westsails were delivered for less money than it cost to build them, and no matter how many boats you sell, you can't make money that way.

They raised the price, but the company's finances were so far behind that it only prolonged the agony. By the middle of 1976, after building more than 800 Westsail 32s, Westsail Corporation declared bankruptcy.

The Westsail showed the yacht business that there was a market for cruising boats that never even pretended to be a racer. It set the stage for all the cruising boats to follow, made by a boatbuilding industry that had been awakened to the existence of a market for cruising sailboats.

On the other side of the country, another big cruising boat entered the market, in 1971, the same year as the Westsail 32. The area around Florida's Tampa Bay, on the Gulf side, was the East Coast analog to Costa Mesa, California. There were lots of small boatbuilders and one of the main players in the boatbuilding scene there was Charley Morgan, who had been building fast, well-designed boats in his St. Petersburg factory. Morgan had begun in 1957 with a 31-foot plywood yawl named *Brisote*, designed with his friend Charlie Hunt. This became, in 1961, *Paper Tiger*, built of fiberglass and famously successful on the Southern Ocean Racing Conference (SORC). Next was a smaller version called the Tiger Cub, but Morgan couldn't find a yard to build it, and so in 1962 he started Morgan Yacht Corporation.

Morgan Yacht did well making racing boats, but saw a market for cruising boats that seemed to have room for another offering. The new design would have a moderate draft to suit the local waters, and also in response to Morgan dealers. They had been asking for roomy boats without the complexity of a centerboard, but with a shallow draft to open up cruising grounds that were off-limits to

The Morgan Out Islander 41 really put Morgan Yachts on the map. Over 1,000 were built, supplying charter fleets and cruisers with a big, stable, comfortable boat. The OI 41, inducted into the Sailboat Hall of Fame in 1996, richly deserves the inclusion. It defined the charter boat, and introduced cruising to people who didn't necessarily want to run off to the South Seas; they just wanted a comfortable boat that was easy to sail and didn't require too many compromises. *Doran Cushing*

14 feet—produced a boat that a sailor's wife could love. Charter companies loved it too. It became the standard charter boat, and with the center cockpit, charter skippers kept the family dry. The center cockpit gave the 41 the feel of a much bigger boat, with a genuine engine room and a luxurious aft cabin.

Initially the 41 had an aft cabin that opened to the deck via a companionway, with a truly big hanging locker to port. When the walk-through model was introduced shortly thereafter, the commodious icebox turned into a nav station and the portside settee and pilot berth became the L-shaped galley. In the aft-cabin version, the U-shaped galley was to starboard and the saloon table was very conventional in appearance, a U-shaped settee that had a dropping table to convert it to a double berth. With the walk-through option, the table was reduced in size, but this opened up the saloon.

Morgan made the change in response to customer requests. The original aft-cockpit boat had accommodations more suitable for a seagoing cruiser, but a lot of 41 sailors apparently were spending more time at anchor or in a marina, where the Out Island 41 Walk-Thru provided a more civilized lifestyle. The entire boat was open, and the people in the aft cabin were able to go forward without going up on deck. The intended market was plain to see from more than the walk-through accommodation plan. "Shag carpet throughout," said the advertisements, not worrying how such floor cover might look after prolonged use by sailors drenched by offshore waves. The shag carpet was a perfect selling point, bringing the civilized comforts of home onto a boat.

The 41 measured 41 feet, 3 inches overall, with a waterline of 34 feet. It was 13 feet, 10 inches on the

the deep-draft racers. The company also sought input from the burgeoning charter boat industry, and the result, in 1971, was the Morgan Out Island 41.

As with the Westsail, it was a boat made for sailors to enjoy. Morgan, like Hunter, also knew that sailboats sell from the inside out, and the 41's beam—2 inches shy of

beam. The keel, unadorned by any "bites," was a full keel in the fullest sense of the word and stuffed with enclosed lead ballast to the tune of 10,500 pounds. The displacement of 24,000 pounds was driven, just, by 774 square feet of working sail, giving a sail area-to-displacement ratio of 14.94, nearly as far off the chart as the Westsail 32's. The two boats had nearly the same beam-to-length ratios, but the 41 weighed less, so its displacement/length was considerably lower, at 273.

A 1971 Morgan sales brochure on the Out Island 41 proclaimed the boat to be "a yacht to him, a home for her, an adventure for all." The brochure was aimed at the husband, assuring him his wife would like the boat. Morgan was selling sizzle too, and it worked.

The 41 came as a ketch or a sloop, but neither boat was known as a windward performer. No matter. Sailors who chartered or bought a 41 weren't going racing; they were going cruising and they wanted comfort, safety, and lots of room.

The Out Island 41 was as big a step in the evolution of cruising sailboats for the masses as the Westsail. The Westsail looked like everyone's vision of a boat. The 41, which was a lot chunkier in profile, didn't have the same visual appeal, but down below, it was comfortable, homelike, even if a bit Spartan. Topside, the 41 was almost a flush-deck boat. Going forward didn't require a tiptoe balancing act on a narrow deck, it was practically a sidewalk.

Charley Morgan retired from boatbuilding the year after the launch of the Out Island 41, but he left a company that had not been "his" since 1968, when Beatrice Foods bought Morgan Yacht Corp. His legacy is the Out Island 41 and the many boats in the Out Island series, from 28 to 51 feet, all developed after the 41 for a market that had been perfectly targeted.

The 41 met the sailing public at the Annapolis Boat Show of 1971, and in 1972 Morgan Yacht built and sold 120 of them. As the demand increased, so did production, until two production lines turned them out at the rate of one a day. Morgan built over 1,000 Out Island 41s, making modifications and slight improvements, but never varying the concept: a solid, comfortable, safe boat that appealed to both halves of the buying public, the husband and the wife. The Morgan Out Island 41 became the most popular boat over 40 feet overall ever built.

With all those big cruising boats being built, what was the sailor of small boats to do? What, especially, was the sailor of trailerable boats to do? Frank Butler knew. He had started a boatbuilding company in 1961, which by 1969 was successful enough that a bigger company bought it. Butler wanted the new company, of which he was now an employee rather than the owner, to build a trailerable 22-foot boat, which he would design. That wasn't a possibility, he was told, and within a year of selling his business, he was fired. This freed him to start another boatbuilding company, this one called Catalina Yachts, to design and build the boat he wanted, a swing-keel, family-sized boat that could be put on a trailer.

Butler began the design project in 1969 and in 1970 his Catalina 22 went into production. Butler, in a message on the Catalina Web site, said he thought that if all went well he hoped to build 100 of them. His new boat, with a fixed keel drawing 3 feet, 6 inches, was 21 feet, 6 inches overall, and 19 feet, 4 inches on the waterline, with a very street-legal beam of 7 feet, 8 inches (federal highway regulations require all highways receiving government money to be wide enough for a trailer 8 feet, 6 inches wide). The Catalina was designed to be a trailer boat, and so the weight was kept down to 2,250 pounds.

It was easy to launch, drawing just 18 inches with the keel up, and carried a modest rig: main and 100 percent jib measured just 212 square feet, giving a sail area-to-displacement ratio of 19.8 (racer-cruiser).

The boats marched out the door in lock step. In 1972, there were 36 boats at the first Catalina 22 regional regatta. By 1973 the first Catalina 22 National Regatta was held, with 45 boats on the starting line.

(opposite) The Catalina 22, a boat design that required the designer to get fired from his job to be built, was the boat that ensured the success of Frank Butler and Catalina Yachts.

Mariah's Eyes

Butler's real talent was in how well he listened to the people who were buying his boats. In 1973 he put a pop-top on the 22, allowing standing headroom when at anchor and the same year he offered a fin keel, increasing the draft to 3 feet, 6 inches. The swing keel, when all the way down, drew 5 feet, by way of comparison. The fin keel added a bit of weight; displacement in that version went up to 2,490 pounds.

Like the Luhrs brothers with the Hunter 25, the first model was such a success that in March 1970 Catalina launched the 27, and in December 1974, the company introduced the tremendously successful Catalina 30.

By this time, the price of fiberglass had begun to climb, and it must have taken both nerve and design cleverness to start building a fiberglass boat. No one was going to build a boat with the scantlings of the Westsail 32, not for the mass market, at any rate. Hulls were built thinner, but with a higher percentage of directional mat,

giving the same strength with less material. Also, the structural qualities of fiberglass were much better understood by the early 1970s, and the resin-to-glass ratio was under better control. It is the glass that provides the strength, after all; the resin merely holds it all together, and, within limits, the less resin, the better.

The 30 had a jaunty look, despite a nearly straight sheerline. The profile was saved by the deckline, which rose steadily from stern to stem, and despite a coachroof tall enough to provide 6 feet, 2 inches of headroom, the 30 refrained from the top-heavy look that sometimes results when a designer tries too hard to enlarge the interior. Indeed, belowdecks the 30 was reputed to have the room of the competition's 34-footers, largely because of the generous beam of 10 feet, 10 inches. A beam-to-length ratio of 2.1 verged on being a radical concept at the time, with the maximum beam roughly 60 percent aft of the bow, but it certainly opened up the saloon.

The Catalina 30 weighed in at 10,200 pounds, with a ballast ratio of slightly over 41 percent and a displacement-to-length ratio of 291. The boat was designed for new sailors, to entice them into a bigger boat that was easy to sail without being intimidating. It must have succeeded, as there are some 7,000 of them on the water.

The standard rig's sail area of 446 square feet is modest, producing a sail area-to-displacement ratio of 15.22 (low, even for a cruiser); with the high ballast ratio, you have a boat that won't be spending a lot of time on its ear. Various versions were soon offered, though, increasing the sail area. The 30 could be ordered with a bowsprit or with a taller rig, or with the tall rig and a bowsprit. The bowsprit allowed a bigger jib, and the 2-foot-taller mast gave some much-needed muscle to the main as well.

As with the cruising boats mentioned above, none of the performance figures seemed to matter with the Catalina 30 customers. They bought a roomy, comfortable, and very affordable boat. Because Catalina was scrupulous about keeping the specs of later models of the C30 consistent with the earlier ones, they inspired a brand loyalty and resale value that is the envy of many of its competitors. Catalina 30 owners race boat-for-boat, and that is the essence of sailboat racing. When they go cruising, they set off in a stable, easily controlled 30-footer with room for the family.

The 30-foot family boat is a hot size. Every boatbuilder wants to have a boat in this size range that does it all—racing, entertaining in the cockpit after the race, cruising, and dinner aboard with the family. They all go about it in slightly different ways. In 1971 Pearson Yachts introduced the Pearson 30, hot on the heels of its successful 26. It's interesting to compare how Pearson went about its 30 and the way the company saw the market compared to Catalina's view of it.

The Pearson 30 was a performance-oriented 30-foot racer-cruiser. The year after its introduction it won the North American three-quarter-ton championship. The Catalina 30 was also a race winner its first year out, taking its class in the Newport-to-Ensenada race—but that is a vastly different achievement.

Being labeled a performance cruiser didn't hurt the Pearson 30 at all. Some families like to sail faster, perhaps, and it was arguably a better boat offshore than the Catalina 30. The P30 was rated with the IOR, something the C30 neither wanted nor aspired to, and still both boats were cruisers, aimed at very similar buyers.

The P30, designed by Bill Shaw, was definitely a racer-cruiser, whereas the P26 was, according to Shaw, a small cruising boat for the inexperienced sailor. The P30 was a race winner that could still be counted on for a family cruise. Pearson sold some 1,185 of the 30-footers—more than 400 of them in 1973 and 1974.

At 29 feet, 10 inches overall, with a waterline length of 25 feet, the P30's measurements were nearly identical to the C30. A look at them both from abeam showed marked differences, though. The Pearson had a noticeable sweep to the sheerline, and the cabintrunk was higher, to give 6 feet, 1 inch of headroom at the

companionway hatch and 5 feet, 11 inches in the saloon. The cabin took up a greater percentage of the P30's overall height amidships, and the lower freeboard gave the P30 a racier look.

Comparing the rest of the numbers shows the P30 displaced nearly a ton less, with just 2 square feet less sail area, so the performance numbers really improved. The P30's sail area-to-displacement is 17.36, at the fast end of the "cruiser" category, and the displacement-to-length ratio is 238, right in the middle of the "light" category.

With 16 inches less beam, at 9 feet, 6 inches, no one would get lost down below, but that slimmer hull was much easier to drive through the water.

The ballast ratio of the P30 is 43 percent, encased internally and glassed in. With a fin keel drawing 5 feet, and the narrow beam, the boat relied much more on ballast than form for stability, so it is initially a bit more tender than the C30. But the P30 soon stiffens up, and its maximum range of positive stability—that is, the angle of heel at which the boat wants to continue going over rather than righting itself—is a very respectable 120 degrees. By way of comparison, the Morgan 41 OI's limit is 105 degrees.

The Pearson 30 was built with strength in mind, explaining why it now shows up in cruising areas far from the California shores where it was built. Below the waterline is a seven-ply lay-up of alternating layers of 1-1/2-ounce mat and 18-ounce roving, with an overlap at the keel, doubling the thickness to over half an inch. The first Catalina 30s had problems with the chainplates (later corrected, with upgrades offered by the factory, typical of Catalina's customer care), but the Pearson's chainplates were bolted to the primary bulkhead and glassed in. The stock Catalina chainplates were undersized and, attached directly to the deck, prone to leaks.

Another difference is the hull-deck join. The Catalina 30 used self-tapping screws at 3-inch intervals and an aluminum rub rail to effect the join, whereas the Pearson glassed the two parts together and used stainless-steel screws on 4-inch centers.

None of the above should be taken to imply that one of these boats is "better" than the other. As with all sailboats, the design and construction should be observed according to how well they function for their intended purpose. Pearson introduced the racer-cruiser concept, and Shaw's P30 resulted in a fast, seaworthy boat.

The Catalina 30, not to put too fine a point on it, was designed more for comfort than for speed, and judging from the numbers, that is what the sailing public wanted.

The first part of the 1970s began with fiberglass still a relatively inexpensive material for boatbuilding. Only four years into the decade, the entire pricing structure on which the industry had been built changed. Rising fiberglass costs, coupled with a short-lived recession, changed the industry.

Manufacturers designed hulls with greater stress analysis, allowing the use of thinner material with equivalent strength. The increased cost of raw materials also spurred the development of new, exotic materials, making boats even lighter and stronger.

The 1970s gave rise to the problem of osmotic blistering of fiberglass hulls as well. This problem, caused by water being absorbed into the hull material, was most serious in boats made during and right after the 1973 petroleum crisis. As Bill Shaw, Pearson's one-time chief designer and general manager, wrote in the *Pearson Current,* "resins were hard to get and manufacturers started to play with formulas and compounds in order to maintain production levels. This did not work out well and has been the major cause of hull blistering."

The mid-1970s wrought nearly as much change on the boatbuilding industry as the introduction of fiberglass three decades earlier, but this change was brought about by pricing shifts rather than a radical new material.

By the 1970s, the type of people who were sailing had firmly and completely changed from the sorts seen on sailboats just 60 years earlier. At the beginning of the century, a high percentage of those who sailed for recreation

were wealthy. As fiberglass boats were built in the hundreds, a market for used boats developed unlike anything seen with wood boats. Fiberglass didn't rot, and repairing boats made of it didn't require a lifetime's worth of skills. Sailors in the 1970s were more likely to work at the factory than own it, and they could own a boat with performance and comfort levels unimaginable to the sailors a generation previous earlier.

With a market that now represented the entire population, designers and builders could work with an economy of scale impossible with wooden boats, regardless of the number built. When you go to your boat broker to look for that next sailboat, whether it is a new one or a used one, the price will reflect all these changes, from design to materials. That puts a lot more of us on the water, sailing the boats that America loves and sails. ✳